John and Mimi Chris

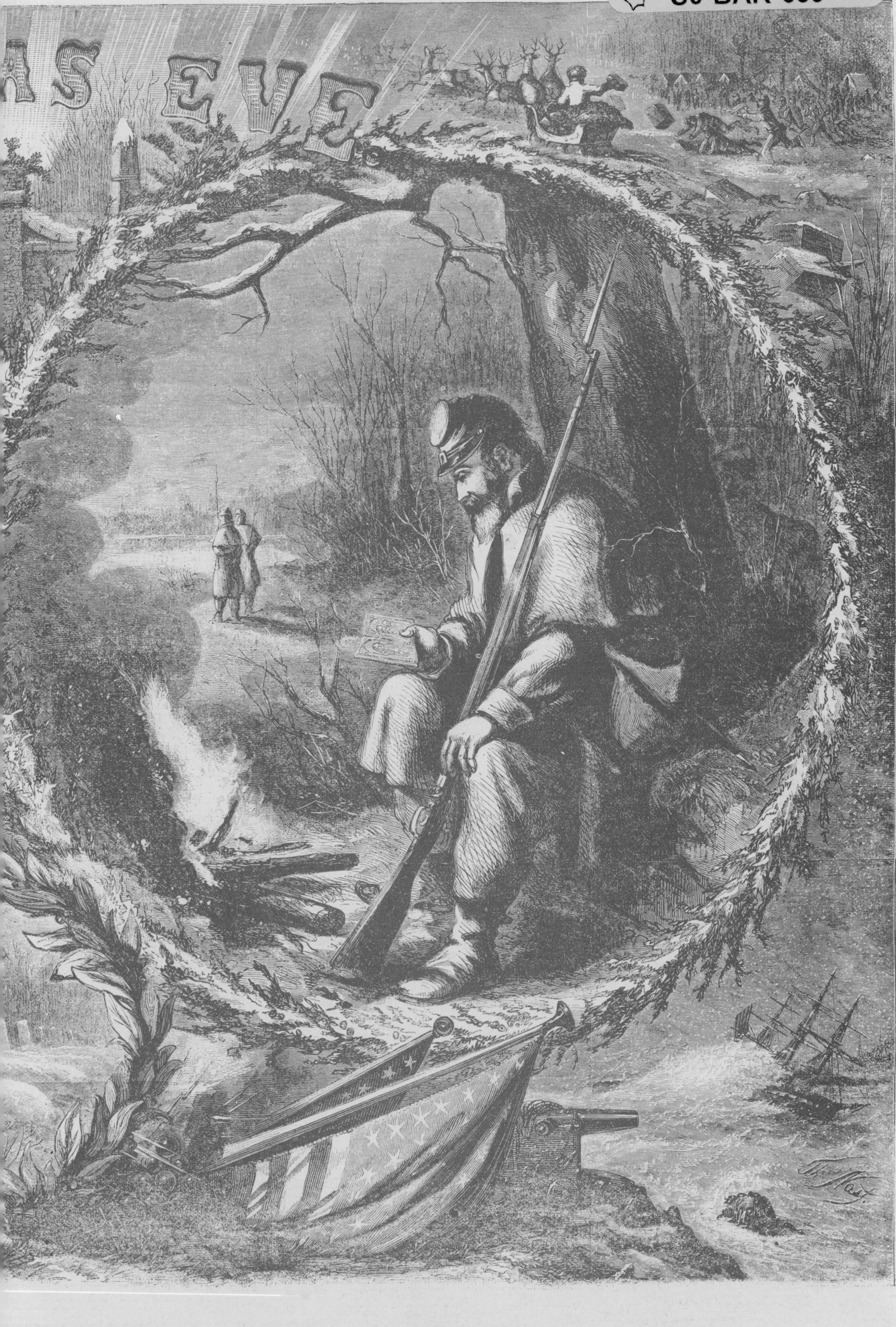

THE CIVIL WAR
CHRISTMAS ALBUM

CHRISTMAS.

The Civil War
CHRISTMAS ALBUM

SELECTED AND EDITED BY

PHILIP VAN DOREN STERN

HAWTHORN BOOKS, INC.

PUBLISHERS · NEW YORK

FIRST EDITION
November, 1961

ACKNOWLEDGMENTS

Most of the pictures in this book came from contemporary engravings in the editor's own collection. Others were obtained from the following: National Archives, Library of Congress, New York Historical Society, Chicago Historical Society, Brooklyn Public Library, New York Public Library, and Nationwide Insurance Companies.

CONTENTS

CONTENTS

CHRISTMAS AT HOME

THE FIRST PEACETIME CHRISTMAS

INTRODUCTION

WHAT WAS CHRISTMAS like during the Civil War? How did people celebrate that holiday a hundred years ago? Did they have Christmas trees and holly? What did they eat for dinner? Did children hang up their stockings for Santa Claus to fill? And what was the status of Santa then? How did he look and what did he do?

Answers to all these questions exist. The people who lived during the Civil War, soldiers and civilians alike, were so attached to the traditional holiday that they left many accounts of it. Other holidays might be forgotten in the stress of wartime, but Christmas was fondly remembered. Soldiers wrote home to tell what happened in field or camp on that day; civilians described the occasion in diaries and journals; artists drew pictures which show us how children, adults, houses, and cities looked. Professional writers contributed stories or poems to the press. And newspapers left a graphic record of the countless little things that make the past seem real.

Some of the best draftsmen of the time prepared sketches to be engraved on woodblocks so they could be printed in illustrated papers like *Harper's* or *Leslie's Weekly.* Winslow Homer drew a number of Christmas pictures; Thomas Nast drew even more. In fact, that uncompromising satirist was so sentimentally attached to Christmas that he collected the drawings he had made on the subject and put them into a book that was brought out toward the end of the century.

But, as was customary then, most artists and writers did their work anonymously. It is quite possible that some of the unsigned pieces printed here are the work of well-known men, but there is no way of identifying them now.

It was to be expected that Christmas would be celebrated widely in this country in the 1860's, for it was then that Santa Claus was reaching his full development as a product of the American imagination. Although his an-

cestry goes back to the fourth century A.D., when a Saint Nicholas flourished in Asia Minor, the Santa Claus we know today first assumed his rotund form in New York early in the nineteenth century. Washington Irving helped to shape him in *A History of New-York,* which he issued under the name Diedrich Knickerbocker in 1809. Then Santa was portrayed in color in a little book printed in New York in 1821. The tiny pages of *The Children's Friend* show him wearing a brown fur hat bearing the legend of "Santeclaus." It also depicts him in a toy-filled sleigh labeled REWARDS which, oddly enough, is drawn by only one reindeer.

Santa, obscurely given form in a book so rare that only two copies are known to exist, was immortalized a year later when Clement C. Moore, also of New York, wrote *Visit from St. Nicholas* for his children. The learned professor, who taught Oriental and Greek literature at the General Theological Seminary, thought so little of the poem that he put it aside. It was published anonymously the next Christmas in the Troy *Sentinel,* but Moore did not acknowledge its authorship until 1837.

Moore gave Santa eight reindeer, which he also named. He sketched a vivid word portrait of Santa's jolly mannerisms, fur costume, pack of toys, and stumpy pipe.

In 1837, the West Point artist, Robert W. Weir (who later painted a portrait of the Military Academy's Superintendent, Colonel Robert E. Lee), made the famous oil painting of Santa standing in front of a fireplace with his sack of toys. Weir's picture reduced Moore's description to visual terms. Our conception of Santa stems from this portrait, which shows the good saint dressed in a red cape trimmed with white fur.

By the time the Civil War came, Santa was a rather well-established figure, who was as popular in the South as in the North. But the North had one great advantage over the South. It had many illustrated periodicals, while the South had very few. As a result, the North was able to capture Santa for the duration, although the South made a valiant attempt to keep his image alive for its children.

This lack of illustrated papers meant that few pictures were made of social activities in the Confederacy during the war. The Union side is much more fully presented. The few Confederate artists who recorded the war concentrated largely on its military aspects. Fortunately, there were many Southerners, women as well as men, who wrote excellent accounts of what went on in those eventful years. Sometimes they wrote about Christmas. Their letters and diaries are especially rich with descriptions of the beloved holiday.

The North, of course, had many other advantages over the South besides the wealth of illustrated material. The North was rich—and rich not only in manpower and weapons but in food and all the good things that do so much to make Christmas a time of feasting and celebration. Although there were many desperately poor people in the North there was never a shortage of food. But as the war dragged on, food grew scarcer in the South, and Christmas became successively leaner each year. People there had to improvise and make do; they thought up all kinds of ingenious substitutes for fancy foods, party decorations, and tree ornaments. But the spirit of Christmas was kept alive, even when parents had to skimp and do without in order that their children might have a happy holiday on the one day of the year that is particularly the children's own.

The picture of Christmas that emerges from contemporary Civil War accounts is a sturdy Victorian one with simple domestic virtues strongly emphasized and traditional customs upheld. The American home—particularly the rural one—illustrated in the Currier and Ives lithographed prints of the period is the ideal setting for a Civil War Christmas. Oddly enough, however, that enterprising firm which did so much to fix the image of mid-nineteenth-century America in the popular mind, printed very few Christmas scenes.

In the field, very little actual fighting was done on Christmas Day. This was not because of religious or sentimental reasons. Major Civil War campaigns usually began in the spring and went on until cold weather closed in, when bad roads and severe weather forced the armies to suspend activities for the winter. A notable exception is Fredericksburg which was fought on December 13, 1862. Even then, however, the fighting was well over by Christmas.

When cold weather set in, the men in both armies began to build huts and cabins to which they added chimneys so a fire could be kept going to warm the interior. The cheerful flames and the cozy glow of the firelight gave these rudely built temporary shelters the illusion of being homes. Undoubtedly they reminded the soldiers of their own true homes and the families they had left behind.

The young men in our Civil War armies were far less sophisticated than their descendants are today. Many of them came from the country; many from large families where domestic relationships were close; nearly all were used to living in big houses where there was plenty of room for parties, for happy celebrations—and for full-sized Christmas trees. To them Christmas had meant a great deal, so they naturally looked back to it wistfully during the war. If there had been a visible index for homesickness it would have soared high over the winter shelters of the dormant armies on Christmas Eve. And on Christmas night, after the feasts and celebrations were over, the lonely men would express their longing for home by singing the carols they had learned in their childhood. Then the voices of men in blue and in gray would sound loud and clear in the cold night air, rising above hill and valley, and drifting out over shell-torn fields where the armies had already fought.

For that evening, at least, the bugles and the guns were stilled, and the centuries-old message went forth: "Glory to God in the highest, and on earth peace, good will toward men."

—PHILIP VAN DOREN STERN

THE CIVIL WAR
CHRISTMAS ALBUM

CHRISTMAS IN THE 1860's

PEACE

The Last Christmas Before the War, December 25, 1860

THIS WAS a deeply troubled and uncertain Christmas, for South Carolina had seceded on December 20, and other Southern states were threatening to follow her out of the Union. And the country was due for another shock on December 26, when Major Robert Anderson suddenly moved his little garrison from Fort Moultrie to Fort Sumter, which commanded the entrance to Charleston Harbor.

The possibility of war was already hurting retail trade on this last peacetime Christmas. The New York *Herald* reported that "People have not got so much money to spend on Christmas presents as in former years, or if they have, they think it more prudent to husband it for expenditures of more real importance." Jewelry sales were down; so were the sales of furs, buffalo robes, and blankets. But toy sales, fortunately, were still good. So were the sales of confectionery.

And the *Herald* commented in an editorial on Christmas Day: "On this Christmas morning we find these states surrounded with perils as terrible as they are unprecedented. The good Ship of State is rushing madly toward the breakers of disunion; the pilot is no longer able to steer his course; already one plank has started; but, thank God, the others still hold. Our best bower anchor, the Constitution, has been let go, and we may yet weather the storm. If not, it will be many a long day before the people of the United States see another merry Christmas.

"While we all should feel a due sense of the responsibility which the present aspect of affairs entails upon each of us, there is still no good reason why we should make ourselves unhappy about it. So the young people shall have their Merry Christmas, and Santa Claus shall be as liberal as ever; the hymn of praise and thanksgiving shall ascend to the Giver of all good; the Christmas tree, the evergreen wreath, the Yule log, the mistletoe bough, all the time-honored symbols of jollity and good cheer, shall be duly honored throughout the length and breadth of this fair land. A right Merry Christmas, then, to all!"

Much to everyone's disappointment, there was no skating in New York on Christmas Day. The weather had been cold, but it had also been so windy that the ice froze in patches, and where it did freeze, its surface was very rough. Fifty-thousand people were reported to have visited Central Park to go skating. When they got to the Park, the red ball that meant good skating was not on display. The suggestion was made that the police at Central Park should telegraph local station houses to display signals hereafter.

In Springfield, where President-elect Abraham Lincoln was whiling away time before his inauguration, there had been a heavy fall of snow. The little city was very quiet, especially around the State House, where the legislators had gone home. The St. Louis *Republican* printed a story about Lincoln:

"An unfortunate man made his appearance here at the police office to solicit money for the purchase of a cork arm. On the 4th of July, while firing a national salute, the cannon prematurely exploded, and the man was very severely injured, losing the use of one eye, and having to have both hands amputated. Several dollars were taken up in his behalf in the police office, and the unfortunate man flourished his hooks in acknowledgment. He stated that the largest contribution which had been taken up for him was at Springfield, Illinois, where he happened to meet Mr. Lincoln.

"Honest Old Abe addressed him as follows: 'Who did you vote for?'

" 'Well,' replied the man, 'to tell the truth, I didn't vote for you. I voted for John Bell.'

"Honest Old Abe said that was right and at once gave the man a twenty-dollar bill, and then collected ten dollars additional from the bystanders."

11

TRINITY CHURCH

CHRISTMAS AT TRINITY

BY CHARLES T. CONGDON

WHILE FROM the lofty gallery sweeps the or-
    gan's music-thunder,
  And rolls a billowy baptism o'er the people
    kneeling under,
Till in the calm that follows the passionate
    prayer abating,
The white-robed priest and white-robed boys
    their praise are alternating;
And through the rosy lattices the golden sun-
    rays clinging,
The marble altars and the walls with love's
    own hue are tinting;
  Down showers tumultuous music from the
    belfry of Old Trinity—
  Merry chiming for His birth, and grave
    songs for His Divinity!

All up and down bright Broadway, with eager,
    festal faces,
In festal garments gayly clad, the population
    paces.
We hear the pulse of one great heart that in
    great love rejoices;
One loving intonation makes a chord of many
    voices;
Upon the long procession, in its coming and
    its going,
Like a river in some fairy land, in Magian
    splendor flowing;
  Down showers tumultuous music from the
    belfry of Old Trinity—
  Merry chiming for His birth, and grave
    songs for His Divinity!

Last night, as by the churchyard, the tombs in
    moonlight sleeping,
I wandered while the shadowed spire across
    the dead was creeping—
Across the dead who pillow'd there, unheed-
    ing gloom or gleaming.
Through all the rolling years have slept the
    sleep that knows no dreaming;
Twelve times the ponderous hammer struck,
    its beat imperious falling:

The dead slept on, and made no sign, but
    waited God's own calling!
  Down showered tumultuous music from the
    belfry of Old Trinity—
  Merry chiming for His birth, and grave
    songs for His Divinity!

There's mockery in our wooing—there is death
    in all our houses;
He liveth best who loveth least—the fool alone
    espouses;
The bridal chaplet that we wear, our brows
    serene adorning,
Fades in the spectral night that dims the eyes
    of dancing morning.
"Sleep well," I cried, "and wisely in your
    graves, O ye departed!
You are blest above the living, for you are
    not broken-hearted!"
  Down showered tumultuous music from the
    belfry of Old Trinity—
  Merry chiming for His birth, and grave
    songs for His Divinity!

Sweet bells of hope! I heard you, with a spirit
    stronger growing,
While over me eternal stars with love and
    strength were glowing;
And when the Christmas noontide came, and
    came the gilded thronging,
I could look on all the happiness nor feel the
    lonesome longing;
While on children lightly leaping, while on
    maid and lover blushing,
While on mothers proud and comely, on the
    living river rushing, ·
  Down showered tumultuous music from the
    belfry of Old Trinity—
  Merry chiming for His birth, and grave
    songs for His Divinity!

From *Harper's New Monthly Magazine.*

SKATING ON THE LADIES' SKATING PON

CENTRAL PARK BY WINSLOW HOMER

CHRISTMAS IN CAMP

THE wintry blast goes wailing by,   Dim forms go flitting through the gloom;
  The snow is falling overhead;   The soldiers cluster round the blaze,
  I hear the lonely sentry's tread,   To talk of other Christmas days,
And distant watch fires light the sky.   And softly speak of home and home.

WAR

Four Wartime Christmases, 1861-1862-1863-1864

THE experiences we have gone through in the foreign wars of the twentieth century tell us little about the realities of a conflict fought on our own soil between our own people. In the Civil War, states became battlegrounds as their citizens wanted to go different ways and families were torn apart.

The first wartime Christmas—1861—was a time when hopes for the new Confederate nation rode high. The South had done well in the year's only major battle, First Bull Run. On November 8, Confederate Commissioners Mason and Slidell were forcibly removed from the British ship *Trent,* and at Christmastime it looked for a while as if Britain might join the Confederacy in a war against the Federal Government.

The second wartime Christmas—1862—was still a time for Southern hopes. At Fredericksburg on December 13, the Confederates, who were strongly entrenched on the heights above the town, hurled back wave after wave of blue-clad troops sent to attack them.

Matters had changed considerably a year later when the third wartime Christmas—1863 —came around. Gettysburg had marked the high tide of Confederate hope, and the fall of Vicksburg had removed the Mississippi River from Confederate control. At Charleston, however, the embattled city and its forts were still holding out.

On Christmas, 1864, a massive two-day combined attack was made on Fort Fisher, the guardian of the Confederacy's last open port, Wilmington, North Carolina. The assault failed, but when it was renewed on January 15, fort and city fell, and the Confederacy no longer had an outlet to the sea.

And so the wartime years passed, filled with sorrow and grief for some and glad victory for others.

Now, a century later, those four war years seem far away. Since then a new world has been born; since then our way of life has changed. The omnipresent automobile has driven the horse from the roads of America, and only in far country places or in a few winter resorts can the sound of sleighbells be heard on a white Christmas. Yet the Christmas that was celebrated then is the kind we would all like to celebrate now. On that magic holiday our thoughts turn to home, and those of us who live in—or can visit—big houses are counted lucky, for it is only in a large house that Christmas is at its best.

In such a house, when there is snow outside, the white winter light is reflected upwards to illuminate ceilings that are ordinarily dark even in strong summer sunlight. Then the rooms are bathed in a soft bluish ambience which means winter and snow and Christmastime. And if there is a fire burning on an open hearth—as there should be, of course—its red and gold hues gleam and dance and flicker on bright surfaces.

And if such a house should be an old one which remembers many Christmases richly garnered through the years, the memories of those who have been happy there return to add joy to the festivities of the day. Then the sorrows of the year—and of all previous years —drop away and are forgotten.

Winter twilight comes, and the room darkens. Candles are brought to add their tiny spheres of glowing magic to the night. Outside, their feet muffled in the snow, the neighbors and their children come to sing Christmas carols.

Some of the songs they sing are very old, so old that they were sung by soldiers on both sides in the Civil War. The men who sang them left an authentic record of their favorite carols, and if you search the pages of this book carefully, you can find out just which ones they preferred.

17

Chicago Historical Society

ROBERT E. LEE WRITES TO HIS WIFE ON CHRISTMAS DAY, 1861

Coosawhatchie, South Carolina
December 25, 1861

I CANNOT let this day of grateful rejoicing pass, dear Mary, without some communication with you. I am grateful for the many among the past that I have passed with you, and the remembrance of them fills me with pleasure. For those on which we have been separated we must not repine. If it will make us more resigned and better prepared for what is in store for us, we should rejoice. Now we must be content with the many blessings we receive. If we can only become sensible of our transgressions, so as to be fully penitent and forgiven, that this heavy punishment under which we labor may with justice be removed from us and the whole nation, what a gracious consummation of all that we have endured it will be!

I am here but little myself. The days I am not here I visit some point exposed to the enemy, and after our dinner at early candle light, am engaged in writing till eleven or twelve o'clock at night.

As to our old home, if not destroyed, it will be difficult ever to be recognized. Even if the enemy had wished to preserve it, it would almost have been impossible. With the number of troops encamped around it, the change of officers, etc., the want of fuel, shelter, etc., and all the dire necessities of war, it is vain to think of its being in a habitable condition. I fear, too, books, furniture, and the relics of Mount Vernon will be gone. It is better to make up our minds to a general loss. They cannot take away the remembrance of the spot, and the memories of those that to us rendered it sacred. That will remain to us as long as life will last, and that we can preserve.

In the absence of a home, I wish I could purchase Stratford. That is the only other place that I could go to, now accessible to us, that would inspire me with feelings of pleasure and local love. You and the girls could remain there in quiet. It is a poor place, but we could make enough corn bread and bacon for our support, and the girls could weave us clothes. I wonder if it is for sale and at how much. Ask Fitzhugh to try to find out, when he gets to Fredericksburg.

You must not build your hopes on peace on account of the United States going into a war with England. She will be very loath to do that, notwithstanding the bluster of the Northern papers. Her rulers are not entirely mad, and if they find England is in earnest, and that war or a restitution of their captives must be the consequence, they will adopt the latter. We must make up our minds to fight our battles and win our independence alone. No one will help us. We require no extraneous aid, if true to ourselves. But we must be patient. It is not a light achievement and cannot be accomplished at once.

I wrote a few days since, giving you all the news, and have now therefore nothing to relate. The enemy is still quiet and increasing in strength. We grow in size slowly but are working hard.

Affectionately and truly,
R. E. LEE

From *Recollections and Letters of General Robert E. Lee* by his son, Captain Robert E. Lee. New York, 1904.

AND TO ONE OF HIS DAUGHTERS

Coosawhatchie,
South Carolina
December 25, 1861

My Dear Daughter:

Having distributed such poor Christmas gifts as I had to those around me, I have been looking for something for you. Trifles even are hard to get these war times, and you must not therefore expect more. I have sent you what I thought most useful in your separation from me and hope it will be of some service. Though stigmatized as "vile dross," it has never been a drug with me. That you may never want for it, restrict your wants to your necessities. Yet how little will it purchase! But see how God provides for our pleasure in every way. To compensate for such "trash," I send you some sweet violets that I gathered for you this morning while covered with dense white frost, whose crystals glittered in the bright sun like diamonds, and formed a brooch of rare beauty and sweetness which could not be fabricated by the expenditure of a world of money.

May God guard and preserve you for me, my dear daughter! Among the calamities of war, the hardest to bear, perhaps, is the separation of families and friends. Yet all must be endured to accomplish our independence and maintain our self-government. In my absence from you I have thought of you very often and regretted I could do nothing for your comfort. Your old home, if not destroyed by our enemies, has been so desecrated that I cannot bear to think of it. I should have preferred it to have been wiped from the earth, its beautiful hill sunk, and its sacred trees buried rather than to have been degraded by the presence of those who revel in the ill they do for their own selfish purposes.

I pray for a better spirit and that the hearts of our enemies may be changed. In your homeless condition I hope you make yourself contented and useful. Occupy yourself in aiding those more helpless than yourself. Think always of your father.

R. E. LEE

CHRISTMAS AT SEA ON ONE OF THE CONFEDERATE RAIDERS

BY RAPHAEL SEMMES

C.S.S. Sumter,
December 25, 1861

CHRISTMAS DAY was passed by us on the lonely sea, in as doleful a manner as can well be conceived. The weather is thus described in my journal: "Thermometer 60°; barometer 29.80. Heavy rain squalls—weather dirty, with lightning all around the horizon, indicating a change of wind at any moment. Under short sail during the night." The only other record of the day was that we "spliced the main brace"; that is, gave Jack an extra glass of grog. Groups of idle sailors lay about the decks, overhauling a range of their memories; how they had spent the last Christmas Day in some Wapping or Wide Water Street, with the brimming goblet in hand, and the merry music of the dance sounding in their ears. Nor were the memories of the officers idle. They clasped in fancy their loved ones, now sad and lonely, to their bosoms once more, and listened to the prattle of the little ones they had left behind.

Not the least curious of the changes that had taken place since the last Christmas Day was the change in their own official positions. They were, most of them, on that day, afloat under the old flag. That flag now looked to them strange and foreign. They had some of their own countrymen on board; not, as of yore, as welcome visitors, but as prisoners. These, too, wore a changed aspect—enemy, instead of friend, being written upon their faces. The two rival nations spoken of by De Tocqueville stood face to face.

From *Service Afloat* by Raphael Semmes. Baltimore, 1887.

WALT WHITMAN SPENDS CHRISTMAS 1862 NEAR FREDERICKSBURG

I WRITE this paragraph in the midst of a large deserted camp ground with the remains of hundreds of mud huts and the debris of an old brigade or division of soldiers all around me. On a road near at hand successive caravans of army wagons, some of them apparently interminable, with their six-mule teams, are passing and passing with only slight intervals nearly all the time. Not far off is a camp of several hundred teamsters with rows and half-moons of wagons ranged around and heaps of forage, hay, temporary stables, etc. In sight, as I sweep my eye over the open ground (for I can see without obstruction from two to four miles every way), I behold several other such teamsters' camps. Off outside, I see the carcasses of dead horses and mules. The wooded parts of the surface have been cleared for fuel and building purposes for a hundred thousand soldiers.

I hear plainly the music of a good band at some Brigadier's quarters a mile and a half away; it is a beautiful, soft, sunny Christmas Day with a thin haze in the air. Then the drum tap from one direction or other comes constantly breaking in.

Where I sit, I am not within many hundred rods of any soldiers' quarters, but I can see them—regiments, brigades, and divisions—spread out in the distance at every point of the compass. All is open ground, not a particle of fence anywhere. Squads of soldiers are wandering, crossing the space, the roads, etc., at a distance, but where I sit, a couple of hundred feet off the road, I am quite solitary.

I am sitting on a remnant of pine log—the old ground site of what was probably a large camp hut. I can see to the southeast the depression in the landscape where the Rappahannock runs, and one or two signs of Fredericksburg (a battery could easily shell it from where I sit). I hear the sound of bugle calls, very martial, at this distance; a fine, large troop of cavalry is just passing; the hoofs of the horses shake the ground, and I hear the clatter of sabers. Amid all this pleasant scene, under the sweet sky and warm sun, I sit and think over the battle of last Saturday week.

CHRISTMAS AT THE FRONT

BY EDWIN FORBES

I WAS just feeling a sense of my own loneliness one Christmas Day when an officer of the Signal Corps invited me to take dinner with some friends of his on the picket line. It was quite early in the morning when we mounted our horses and started from camp. After riding some miles, we came in sight of the picket reserves; then rode on and found that the main picket line extended across a valley through which flowed a creek. Nearing a point of crossing, we passed a picket post on a sandbar in the middle of the stream, and halted to admire the beautiful surroundings. The hut, which was prettily fashioned of pine boughs, sheltered three or four sleeping men, while the cook was getting a frugal dinner ready on the campfire in front. Nearby, the officers' mess was being prepared, and we were cordially invited to partake of "chicken fricassee, camp-style." The odor of the cooking was appetizing, and our long ride had given us an appetite, but as we were expected elsewhere, we were obliged to decline and soon took leave of the hospitable officers.

We rode down the line and found the post, commanded by my comrade's friend, on an old farm road. The men were camped in the farm garden, where they had thrown up a shelter of boards against the fence as a protection from the cold wind. We dismounted in the barnyard, and entrusted our horses to an old Negro servant who promised them a feed of corn. We were most cordially received, and the dinner was soon placed before us on a

A CHRISTMAS DINNER

Library of Congress

table improvised from the cover of an oat-bin.

We found that living on the outer picket line was much better than in the main army camp, and were surprised at the real luxuries placed before us, most of which had been obtained from the farmers at very small cost. The bill of fare consisted of rabbit stew, fricasseed chicken, griddle cakes with honey, and excellent coffee. To this we did full justice, and, with the addition of a little "commissary," had a more enjoyable feast than we had eaten in months.

After an hour or two of social chat over our pipes, we rode farther down the line and stopped at various points to talk with friends who were on duty. None seemed to have fared as sumptuously as ourselves; most of the men were cooking salt pork, though one party had secured a turkey from a neighboring farmer and looked lovingly towards it as it roasted before the glowing campfire. Some of the men were fortunate enough to have received boxes from home, and their faces grew bright as they lifted out roast turkey, chickens, bread, cake and pies that kindly hands had prepared. An occasional bottle of "old rye," secreted in a turkey or loaf of bread, would give rise to much fun and expected enjoyment. The provost guard, however, seldom overlooked a bottle, and confiscated any contraband liquor; and his long experience had bred in him a sort of special sense for any such little infractions of the rule, which was inflexible even for Christmas, and if got the better of at all had to be by a skillful and imperceptible breaking.

But little more of interest came in our way on the agreeable trip I have mentioned, and we returned to camp much brightened by the scenes which so pleasantly broke the monotony of soldier life on that Christmas Day at the front.

From *An Artist's Story of the Great War* by Edwin Forbes. New York, 1890.

A CONFEDERATE'S REMINISCENCE OF CHRISTMAS, 1861

BY W. F. SHIPPEY, C.S.A.

IT WAS CHRISTMAS DAY in the year 1861. A party of officers and soldiers of the old First Virginia Cavalry, then encamped near Bull Run, had assembled to celebrate the day at Stuart's Tavern on the Little River Turnpike. The day was cold and dark and dreary, but the bright fire from the old-fashioned fireplace, shining upon the polished andirons, sanded floor, and cheerful faces of mine host and his guests in their gray uniforms and their burnished side arms leaning conveniently in the corners of the room, gave an air of comfort and snugness to the scene which contrasted favorably with the outdoor gloom, and gave something like a home feeling to the soldiers who, for several months, had known nothing better than a fly tent, or a crossroads bivouac.

Our horses were picketed at the front fence, ready to mount and away should any foraging party of the enemy happen along and disturb us in our festivities, but we trusted to the inclemency of the weather and proximity of our infantry pickets to prevent any such interruption, but the rule of our lives in the front under Jeb Stuart was vigilance, and on this occasion it was not relaxed.

With song and jest and story interspersed with occasional libation to the shrine of Bacchus (represented by a large bowl of punch and an eggnog on the center table), the hours passed merrily away while the landlord busied himself with preparations for dinner, and the odor of roast turkey and other good things from the kitchen sharpened the already keen appetites of the hungry soldiers.

In the midst of this scene of enjoyment, a solitary horseman rode up to the house, dismounted and entered—a tall soldierly looking man in uniform of a captain of infantry. Seeing that we were a private party and believing himself to be an intruder, he was about to beat a retreat, but we pressed him to join us, and after some hesitation he consented to do so. He introduced himself as Captain Atkins of

Wheat's battalion and told us that the battalion was on picket duty, and he on the grand round, and had come out of his way to warm himself by the hospitable fireside of the tavern. Learning from him that Major Wheat was on the line, Meade and I started off in search of him. We found him at his headquarters, a fly tent under a tree at the crossroad, and it required no great deal of eloquence to induce him to join our dinner party.

In fancy I can see the happy faces that gathered around the table and responded to the toast, "Our Dixie Land." Alas! ere another Christmas had come around some of them had paid the soldier's debt. The memory of those days seems like a beautiful dream seen through the mists of the rolling years. We were boys then, fired with enthusiasm and ardor in the cause we loved so much. The dark side of war had not dimmed the halo that invested all things with a beautiful romance. Up to that time we had known no such word as defeat. The victories of Bull Run and Manassas, and several small cavalry fights, had given us prestige, and we gloried in our colors and our chief. The cypress had not become so entwined with the laurel as to dim the luster of our chaplets, and cause us to mingle tears with our songs of triumph; and victory was the watchword of those who followed the feather of Stuart.

The dinner passed pleasantly without interruption, and the stars had set their sentinel watch in the sky when we parted and made our way back to camp, filled with enthusiasm, turkey, and punch, to say nothing of eggnog, oysters, and many other delicacies provided by our host. Indeed, so happy were we, that we found some difficulty in getting back to camp, though the road was plain, and there were few paths in the country around Manassas unknown to Stuart's Cavalry. They had learned them all, as the infantry would say, in buttermilk ranging.

Southern Historical Society Papers, Vol. II, 1883.

THE CHRISTMAS AFTER FREDERICKSBURG

AFTER the battle of Fredericksburg the fine weather, clear, cold and bracing, which we had been having, changed into a real Virginia winter with a good deal of the Northern thrown in. It snowed, froze, thawed and rained by turns, with here and there bright days. All military operations were brought to a close, and both armies went into winter quarters.

Every style of camp architecture was to be found, including hut, hovel, shack and shed, and every other plan of building that limited genius could devise. Officers and men messed together; therefore their style of tabernacle was no better than ours. Some energetic fellows worked like beavers and erected a good substantial log house with fine chimney and canvas roof, snug, airtight and rainproof.

Some of the huts were large and roomy, holding a mess of a dozen comfortably; others were of a size capable of accommodating three or four, while here and there one would come across a modern Diogenes who dug some hole in which he proposed to drag out the winter by himself.

The latter part of December was fearful; a long rain followed the battle, then a hard, bitter freeze came. So intense was the cold that the men did nothing but cower over the fire piled high with wood night and day, or keep snugged up under blankets, which in such weather rose in value to a thousand dollars a square inch. The earth was frozen as hard as granite; the streams were solid: Ice King held all nature in a relentless grasp.

All drills, inspections and even guard mountings were suspended during this freezing weather. A man hardly dared poke his nose out of the tent, except to go for wood and water and to draw his rations.

Then came on a thaw for three or four days, with really warm weather, when everything melted; when the streams burst their bonds; when the earth became soft until it seemed to have no bottom and mud reigned supreme. It was everywhere; the roads were almost impassable and it was difficult to haul the rations to camp from the station. A detail of seventy-five was made from the Seventeenth to assist the brigade wagons back to camp.

It was a cheerless task. The heavy army wagons came toiling laboriously along; many became stalled in the mud, the wheels sunken below the hubs, horses straining, the drivers cursing and lashing the poor animals, while a dozen men pushed at each wheel, all and everything covered with the liquid mire; such was December in Virginia.

The Christmas of 1862 was cheerless indeed; the weather was frightful, and a heavy snowstorm covered everything a foot deep. Each soldier attempted to get a dinner in honor of the day, and those to whom boxes had been sent succeeded to a most respectable degree, but those unfortunates whose homes were outside the lines had nothing whatever delectable partaking of the nature of Christmas. Well! it would have puzzled [anyone] to furnish a holiday dinner out of a pound of fat pork, six crackers, and a quarter of a pound of dried apples. We all had apple dumplings that day, which with sorghum molasses were not to be despised.

Some of the men became decidedly hilarious, and then again some did not; not because they had joined the temperance society nor because they were opposed to the use of intoxicating liquors, but because not a soul invited them to step up and partake. One mess in the Seventeenth did not get so much as a smell during the whole of the holidays; and a dry, dismal old time it proved.

We read in the Richmond papers of the thousands and thousands of boxes that had been passed en route to the army, sent by the ladies of Richmond and other cities, but few found their way to us. The greater part of them were for the troops from the far South who were too distant from their homes to receive anything from their own families. The Virginians were supposed to have been cared for by their own relatives and friends; but some of them were not, as we all know.

From *Johnny Reb and Billy Yank* by Alexander Hunter, C.S.A. New York, 1905.

CHRISTMAS BOXES IN CAMP—CHRISTMAS, 1861, BY WINSLOW HOMER

A UNION SOLDIER'S SECOND CHRISTMAS IN DIXIE

BY LAWRENCE VAN ALSTYNE

December 24, 1863

As TOMORROW is Christmas we went out and made such purchases of good things as our purses would allow, and these we turned over to George and Henry for safe keeping and for cooking on the morrow. After that we went across the street to see what was in a tent that had lately been put up there. We found it a sort of show. There was a big snake in a showcase filled with cheap looking jewelry, each piece having a number attached to it. Also, a dice cup and dice. For $1.00 one could throw once, and any number of spots that came up would entitle the thrower to the piece of jewelry with a corresponding number on it.

Just as it had all been explained to us, a greenhorn-looking chap came in and, after the thing had been explained to him, said he was always unlucky with dice, but if one of us would throw for him he would risk a dollar just to see how the game worked. Gorton is such an accommodating fellow I expected he would offer to make the throw for him, but as he said nothing, I took the cup and threw seventeen. The proprietor said it was a very lucky number, and he would give the winner $12 in cash or the fine pin that had the seventeen on it. The fellow took the cash, like a sensible man. I thought there was a chance to make my fortune and was going right in to break the bank, when Gorton, who was wiser than I, took me to one side and told me not to be a fool; that the greenhorn was one of the gang, and that the money I won for him was already his own. Others had come by this time and I soon saw he was right, and I kept out. We watched the game a while, and then went back to Camp Dudley and to bed.

Christmas, and I forgot to hang up my stocking. After getting something to eat, we took stock of our eatables and of our pocket books, and found we could afford a few things we lacked. Gorton said he would invite his horse jockey friend, James Buchanan, not the ex-President, but a little bit of a man who rode the races for a living. So taking Tony with me I went up to a nearby market and bought some oysters and some steak. This with what we had on hand made us a feast such as we had often wished for in vain. Buchanan came, with his saddle in his coat pocket, for he was due at the track in the afternoon. George and Henry outdid themselves in cooking, and we certainly had a feast. There was not much style about it, but it was satisfying. We had overestimated our capacity, and had enough left for the cooks and drummer boys. Buchanan went to the races, Gorton and I went to sleep, and so passed my second Christmas in Dixie.

At night the regiment came back, hungry as wolves. The officers mostly went out for a supper, but Gorton and I had little use for supper. We had just begun to feel comfortable. The regiment had no adventures and saw no enemy. They stopped at Baton Rouge and gave the 128th a surprise. Found them well and hearty, and had a real good visit. I was dreadfully sorry I had missed that treat. I would rather have missed my Christmas dinner. They report that Colonel Smith and Adjutant Wilkinson have resigned to go into the cotton and sugar speculation. The 128th is having a free and easy time, and according to what I am told, discipline is rather slack. But the stuff is in them, and if called on every man will be found ready for duty. The loose discipline comes of having nothing to do. I don't blame them for having their fun while they can, for there is no telling when they will have the other thing.

From *Diary of an Enlisted Man* by Lawrence Van Alstyne. New Haven, Conn., 1910.

CHRISTMAS

44th Regt.

EXCELSIOR

HALL

A REGIMENT

CHRISTMAS CELEBRATION

THE LONE SENTRY

A COLD CHRISTMAS IN THE SHENANDOAH VALLEY IN 1864

OUR CAMP at Charlestown was on ground made historic not only by its former ownership by Charles, the younger brother of George Washington, and by having been for a time the resting place of Braddock's boastful army, but also by the trial and execution here of John Brown. The house in which we were entertained was once the home of Samuel Washington, elder brother of George, and many men known to fame have enjoyed its hospitality, among them Louis Philippe—afterwards King of France—and his younger brothers the Duke de Montponsier and the Count de Beaujolaix.

The rest of the winter would have been passed quietly in the Valley but for the desire of General Grant to have the railroads about Gordonsville destroyed. To this end we were awakened at half-past four o'clock on the 19th of December—a cold, dismal, rainy morning—and ordered to put up four days' rations and forage, and to be ready to move at six. The expedition consisted of two divisions of cavalry—Merritt's and Powell's, in all about 5000 men and 24 wagons—and made a column about five miles long, under the command of General Torbert. . . .

We took the direction of Front Royal. It was a very picturesque sight to look back from some commanding hill and see the column winding like an immense serpent through the Valley. After we passed Front Royal we began to ascend the western slope of the Blue Ridge, and when we had penetrated about halfway through Chester Gap, we were halted for the night. And such a night! A bleaker camp could not be imagined. The winter as a whole was exceptionally severe for Virginia, snow falling frequently, and the mercury sinking sometimes to zero. It was excruciating at the climax of this inclement season to be perched at the top of a pass in the Blue Ridge and to face the icy blasts as they sucked and swirled through the narrow gorge. We made a large fire of logs, and after a supper of hard bread and coffee, lay down upon blankets,

with our saddles for pillows, and our feet towards the fire, which the guard was directed to keep bright. . . . Reveille at five was a relief—anything rather than stay longer upon those cold heights in the clouds. We descended the eastern slope of the Blue Ridge and were soon in a warmer atmosphere. Our course was now southwest, right under the Ridge and hugging it all the way. We made about 35 miles between sunrise and sunset, halting for ten minutes every two hours. That night it threatened rain and I went . . . under a shelter tent and had a good sleep till 4:30, when to our great surprise we waked to find four inches of snow on the ground. . . . Early in the day the storm changed from snow to sleet and then to a very cold rain, and as we dismounted to rest our horses we wet our feet and could not get them warm again.

We halted at four o'clock on the summit of one of a circle of hills encompassing the town of Criglersville, and there I beheld the grandest cloud scenery that I had ever witnessed. The whole valley was a vast amphitheatre in the hills, whose sides and summits were heavily hung with thick clouds big with storm and tempest. The firmament . . . was perfectly clear, and we stood upon the one elevation of all around that was open to the eye of heaven. It was very grand, but I have enjoyed the pictured memory of it more than I did the actual sight, as I was suffering so much from the cold. . . . As we descended from this summit, it grew colder, and before we had gone many miles, the ground was frozen and our ears and feet almost so.

We soon approached Madison Court House, and here we first struck the enemy and skirmished. . . . It was a bitterly cold and most cheerless hour. The thought of the night before us was enough to freeze the blood. But soon the order came to fall back into the woods and encamp. Fortunately it was a pine forest into which we now entered, and the thick boughs broke the force of the wind. We cut down small pine trees and taking their flat-spreading branches laid them upon the snow for a bed, and then built a fire and surrounded ourselves with a barricade of boughs stuck in the snow. It was eleven o'clock before we had supper, and as we had not eaten anything since six in the morning, of course we were very hungry. That night we had a splendid sleep. Pine boughs were as grateful as mattresses to our chilled and tired frames. We slept within two feet of the fire and so kept warm.

Five hours of rest, and reveille called us to go again on our journey. We passed through Madison Court House and took the road to Gordonsville. It was very cold, and the horses slipped round on the frozen snow like hogs on ice. But we pressed on to the Rapidan, broke through the ice and forded the river, and made a reconnaissance towards Gordonsville, driving in the enemy's advance guards and capturing . . . two pieces of artillery. In this way we discovered that reinforcements had already reached Gordonsville from Richmond, and that the place was too strong to be attacked. We also learned that Wharton's division of infantry had been detached from Early's forces at Staunton in order to check Torbert, and that they were approaching by way of Charlottesville. So we were forced to give up the object of the expedition and to retreat as fast as possible. That night we encamped again in the woods the same way as the night before, only we had become so chilled through the exposures of the day that it was almost impossible to get warm. The nearer I got to the fire, the more I would shiver. My blood seemed curdled with the cold, and as it crept slowly through my veins, made me shake in every fiber.

Friday, December 23, reveille sounded at five again, and with a breakfast of coffee alone, we started. Our rations and forage were now exhausted, and for the rest of our journey we must live on the country. In the course of the day our headquarters forager brought in two hams, a spare-rib, and enough flour for several days. We marched until eleven o'clock that night, and encamped under the cold light of stars on a side hill so steep that we had to crawl on our hands and knees to keep from falling. The top of the snow was frozen into a hard crust which the horses' hoofs scarcely broke. However, we made ourselves comfortable with a log fire, a supper of coffee, ham, and griddle cakes, and a bed of boughs, and after five hours we started again.

Our regimental position this day was in the rear of the column, a very uncomfortable place to be in when the column is long and the roads are bad. There were many places where an obstruction or break in the road made it impossible for more than two horses to pass abreast; and as we generally marched by fours, the column at such places would be drawn out to twice its normal length; and if the advance moved steadily it would get away eight or ten miles from the rear at such an obstruction, and then the rear companies, after having waited to let the others pass the obstacle, would have to gallop to close up the column. Generally, however, at such a place, the advance waits for the rear to catch up, as a caterpillar when it meets an obstruction huddles up, fixes its tail, then lengthens out over the obstacle, fixes its head and, drawing in its lengthened body, huddles up again and then creeps on as before with equal length. Besides this unevenness of motion, a position in the rear is also unpleasant from the sights one has to witness. On this day we passed hundreds of horses worn out by the toilsome march and left dead by the side of the road; and we kept passing dismounted men who could not keep up with the column, some of them with boots worn through and a few barefoot and leaving tracks of blood in the frozen crust. That night we got into camp at nine o'clock, cold, tired, and hungry; still we brightened up a little to think it was Christmas Eve, and that our friends at home were enjoying it in quiet comfort and happy meetings, even though we could not enjoy it, but must spread our cold and cheerless tables in the presence of those enemies who otherwise would make our home firesides cold and cheerless as our own.

Next day was Sunday, December 25th, and as we woke, the "Merry Christmas" wishes went around, but always with the added wish for a merrier Christmas next year.

We forded this day the two branches of the Rappahannock, having first to cut a passage through the ice that covered the river.

In our march we often had to dismount and to lead our horses down the steep hills, sliding with them most of the way. Their shoes were now so smooth that they with difficulty kept from falling even on level ground. Our sufferings this day from the cold were very severe. Our feet were almost frozen, encased as they were in wet and frozen boots, and dangling in the frosty air. There is not sufficient exercise in the slow motion of a cavalry column to send the warm blood away down to the feet. Our only relief was a partial one when the column halted—in stamping upon the ground.

Next day—December 26th—we passed through Sulphur Springs, whose once magnificent hotel, where the beauty and chivalry of Virginia used to gather and revel, was now a mass of ruins, and the place was almost utterly deserted. We drank of the waters, without however renewing our youth. . . . As we passed through Warrenton, General Torbert narrowly escaped being killed by a shot fired by a guerrilla from some safe concealment. Leaving Warrenton, we took the road to White Plains, and went into camp in that region infested with guerrillas.

Next day—December 27th—we marched through Middleburg and Upperville, and recrossed the Blue Ridge at Ashby's Gap, being fired upon several times by guerrillas concealed in the woods. We forded the Shenandoah with difficulty in its winter flood, and went into camp on its north bank at ten o'clock. After we got asleep a heavy rain began to fall, and I awoke at three o'clock to find myself lying in a puddle of water safely held in the hollows of my rubber blanket. I got up and readjusted it and lay down again, but was too chilled to sleep.

An early breakfast and a short march brought us back to our old camps near Winchester, thankful to have escaped from the hardships and exposures of the hardest expedition of the war with only a few painful reminders of it in chilblains, shivers, and twinges of rheumatism.

From *Field, Camp, Hospital and Prison in the Civil War, 1863–1865* by Charles A. Humphreys. Boston, Mass., 1918.

A CHRISTMAS LEGEND OF LOOKOUT MOUNTAIN

BY CAPTAIN DAVID A. MURPHY

A SOUTHERN belle, unhors'd, alone,
    on Lookout Mountain's crest;
From frightened steed she had been thrown
    —half conscious, but distressed.
Bruised and bleeding on the ground,
    she wept her plight till she was found.

Orphan for years, her mountain home
    Not half a mile away,
No fairer maid 'neath heaven's dome
    Than witching Lucille Clay.
While riding home her saddle turned,
The mettled horse its burden spurned.

A captain bold, from Vermont State,
    His camp was strolling 'round;
He found her there in anguish great,
    Helpless and on the ground.
His blue coat placed beneath her head,
She swooned, and woke as from the dead.

He was attached to Hooker's corps,
    In heart and fancy free;
Her beauty won, 'midst war's uproar,
    His love and sympathy.
Proffered his aid with no delay,
With scorn she tossed his coat away.

And then she spoke, proudly irate,
    "I hate you and your blue.
I love the South; whate'er my fate
    No help seek I from you!"
She sought to rise, but sank in pain;
His duty then was doubly plain.

Quickly his dog dispatched to camp—
    Rover, well trained and wise—
An ambulance—the weather damp—
    Brought surgeon and supplies.
His captive fair, Miss Lucille Clay;
But captured square, Sir Lucien Gray.

Her uncle's home, in half an hour,
    Held lady and her guest;
Safe within her beauty bower

She found relief and rest.
The parting proved two points of view:
"I hate you, *Sir!*" "I don't hate *you!*"

The war progressed from East to West;
  Grant's armies swarmed like bees;
In valleys deep, on mountains' crest,
  Brave men were felled like trees.
Lucille once dreamed, 'midst hopes and fears,
The captain slain; she woke in tears.

War's moons had waned, peace blest the land,
  Joyous was the rebound.
The battles fought on Lookout grand
  Made that mount famous ground.
On Pulpit Rock, one summer day,
They met by chance, nor ran away.

Lucille was sweet, and seemed surprised;
  Lucien was frank and bold.
Hero he stood and well devised
  His love with fervor told.
But she refused his heart and name,
Her Southern pride chiefly to blame.

He woo'd to win; the siege was strong;
  His form she hated not.
The struggle fierce and lasted long;
  Beleaguered was her lot.
He roamed all roads—heart spake through
    eyes,
The mount to *him,* love's Paradise.

He fain must win who dares to wait.
  Justice would have it so.
Gibraltar sieged but tempts its fate;
  Pride's walls shall be laid low.
Four, eight, twelve moons he stood his
    ground;
Though baffled oft, at length was crowned.

Not as man planned but as God willed,
  One fateful Christmas day,
Thrown by his horse, his pulse seemed stilled,
  So breathless there he lay.
His steed's foot struck an army shell,
Plunged forward, and on rider fell.

The faithful dog his mission knew;
  To Lucille straightway sped;
His howls and whines her presence drew;

She followed where he led.
She found Gray prone on the same spot
Where Cupid's bow the captain shot.

O'er him she stooped, she kissed his face,
  Her lap pillowed his head;
Tears whelmed her pride, she prayed for
    grace,
  "I'll die if he be dead!"
His careful nurse, she saved his life;
The Northman won his Southern wife.

Two children grow in Tennessee,
  Fruit of their wedded joys;
The first named GRANT, the second LEE,
  And both are Union boys.
Gray's happy home seems youth's fountain;
Christmas o'ertops Lookout Mountain.

Grant spoke to Lee on New Year's Day;
  "Let us have peace!" said he.
"And love," said Lee, "for blue and gray,
  We're both, it seems to me."
The captain asked in merriment,
"Lucille, *which* shall be President?"

From the magazine *Blue and Gray,* January, 1895.

A UNION NURSE GETS
AN UNUSUAL
CHRISTMAS PRESENT

IN PENNSYLVANIA and New Jersey State quarters combined, we had three good-sized connecting tents; and later the little New York house was added.

Our kitchen was generally run by Hannah, a rather incompetent contraband with great wondering eyes and slipshod feet. There were many such about camp, girls and women as well as men and boys—anxious to work for shelter and food, but without knowledge of the value of money, which they generally squandered at the sutler's for some trifle such as candy or something to eat.

A good cooking stove was a great comfort, and Doctor Painter, an excellent cook, made our mess appetizing. The agents were expected to get their sustenance from state sup-

WINTER QUARTERS IN CAMP

plies, and we could buy from the Commissary Department good bread and coffee. Our table was made of boards resting on barrels, and sometimes we were quite stylish, having a white tablecloth instead of newspapers. Our dishes, mostly of tin, served quite well for hungry hurried appetites.

Our reception tent, which was the largest, had at first a bunk in one corner where the rain sometimes percolated through the canvas walls, and one morning—my pillow touching the wet wall of the tent—I found my head in a little puddle of water. But I was in better health, if possible, than before. We laughed at these happenings also when the rain ran in streams over our ground floor and at night we were obliged to sit resting or writing by the light of candles stuck in bottles with our feet on logs to keep them dry. Meanwhile a log fire burned cheerfully in the rough mud and log chimney. A barrel was placed on top for draught. It sometimes caught fire, but some-

one always managed to discover it and knocked it off without setting fire to the canvas roofs. Our barrel chairs were not luxurious, but like everything in camp, they served their purpose.

Though our tents were not transparent, the candle distinctly silhouetted our forms on the walls as we sat talking with friends, so that passers could recognize visitors and perhaps wait for a more favorable time to call. During the day our tent flaps were always open hospitably. Agents and officers often visited and talked of home, friends, comforts, etc., while each was always ready to assist in an emergency. Convalescents often got leave to come for some luxury or necessity; they craved fruit and vegetables, especially onions, and one so craved this luxury that he offered me fifty cents for one. Of course it became a gift, and one that was greatly enjoyed.

On Christmas Day, 1864, Mrs. Painter, wishing to make a pleasant surprise with

33

home-made cheer for her son, Hettit K. Painter, who was still in charge of the telegraph at Hatch's Run, invited me to accompany her.

After the usual bumping over corduroy and other bad roads near the point, we found him in his little improvised office and living room. Doctor Painter with the assistance of a cheerful contraband helper soon prepared a surprisingly comfortable Christmas dinner, which was greatly enjoyed by our little party.

During this homely visit, Hettie Painter remarked to me, "Miss Smith, you are always looking up some souvenir of the war. Here is something that you may appreciate. This is a telegram from General Sherman received here this morning en route, and I immediately forwarded a copy to President Lincoln in Washington. It is therefore a copy of the message before it was dispatched to the President."

Much pleased with this souvenir, now a relic of that wonderful conquest, I have preserved it carefully. The following is a verbatim copy:

> The United States Military Telegraph
> Savannah, Ga., 23, 1864
> Via Fortress Monroe, 25

To his Excellency, President Lincoln:

I beg leave to present you as a Christmas gift the City of Savannah, 150 guns and plenty of ammunition; also about twenty-five thousand bales of cotton.

> W. T. Sherman
> Major-General

I mailed it to my home, writing on the back, "This dispatch was just received by a telegraph reporter. It is the first reliable original telegram."

From *Reminiscences of an Army Nurse during the Civil War* by Adelaide W. Smith. New York, 1911.

A CONSCRIPT'S CHRISTMAS

BY JOEL CHANDLER HARRIS

ON a Sunday afternoon in December, 1863, two horsemen were making their way across Big Corn Valley in the direction of Sugar Mountain. They had started from the little town of Jasper early in the morning, and it was apparent at a glance that they had not enjoyed the journey. They sat listlessly in their saddles, with their carbines across their laps, and whatever conversation they carried on was desultory.

The journey from Jasper to the top of Sugar Mountain was not a pleasant one even in the best of weather, and now, with the wind pushing before it a bitterly cold mist, its disagreeableness was irritating. And it was not a short journey. Big Corn Valley was fifteen miles across as the crow flies, and the meanderings of the road added five more. Then there was the barrier of the foothills and finally Sugar Mountain itself, which when the weather was clear lifted itself above all the other mountains of that region.

Nor was this all. Occasionally, when the wind blew aside the oilskin overcoats of the riders, the gray uniform of the Confederacy showed beneath. They wore cavalry boots, and there were tell-tale trimmings on their felt hats. With these accoutrements to advertise them, they were not in a friendly region. There were bushwhackers in the mountains, and the fodder stacks in the valley that rose like huge and ominous ghosts out of the mist might conceal dozens of guerrillas. They had that day ridden past the house of the only member of the Georgia State convention who had refused to affix his signature to the Ordinance of Secession, and the woods were full of Union men.

Suddenly one of the horsemen drew rein. "Where does this cussed road lead to anyhow?"

"To the mountain—straight to the mountain," grimly remarked the other, who had stopped to see what was the matter with his companion.

"Great Jerusalem! straight? Do you see that fodder stack yonder with the hawk on the top

of the pole? Well, we've passed it four times, and we ain't no further away from it now than we was at fust."

"Well, we've no time to stand here. In an hour we'll be at the foot of the mountain, and a quarter of a mile further we'll find shelter. We must attend to business and talk it over afterwards."

"An' it's a mighty nice business, too," said the man who had first spoken. He was slender in build, and his thin and straggling mustache failed to relieve his effeminate appearance. He had evidently never seen hard service. "I never have believed in this conscriptin' business," he went on in a complaining tone. "It won't pan out. It has turned more men agin the Confederacy than it has turned fer it, or else my daddy's name ain't Bill Chadwick, nor mine neither."

"Well," said the other curtly, "it's the law,

Bill Chadwick, and it must be carried out. We've got our orders."

"Oh, yes! You are the commander, Cap'in Moseley, an' I'm the army. Ain't I the gayest army you ever had under you? I'll tell you what, Cap'in Moseley (I'd call you Dick, like I useter, if we wasn't in the ranks), when I j'ined the army I thought I was goin' to fight the Yankees, but they slapped me in the camp of instruction over there at Adairsville, an' now here we are fightin' our own folks. If we ain't fightin' 'em, we are pursuin' after 'em, an' runnin' 'em into the woods an' up the mountains. Now what kind of a soldier will one of these conscripts make? You needn't tell me, Cap'in! The law won't pan out."

"But it's the law," said Captain Moseley. The captain had been wounded in Virginia, and was entitled to a discharge, but he accepted the position of conscript officer. He

35

had the grit and discipline of a veteran, and a persistence in carrying out his purposes that gave him the name of "Hardhead" in the army. He was tall and muscular, but his drooping left shoulder showed where a Federal ball had found lodgment. His closely cropped beard was slightly streaked with gray, and his face would have been handsome had not determination left its rude handwriting there.

The two rode on together in silence a little space, the cold mists, driven by the wind, tingling in their faces. Presently Private Chadwick resumed the thread of his complaints.

"They tell me," he said, "that it's a heap easier to make a bad law than it is to make a good one. It takes a lot of smart men a long time to make a good one, but a passel of blunderbusses can patch a bad one up in a little or no time. That's the way I look at it.

"What's the name of this chap we are after? Israel Spurlock? I'd like to know, by George, what's the matter with him! What makes him so plague-taked important that two men have to be sent on a wild-goose chase after him? They yerked him into the army, an' he yerked himself out, an' now the word is that the war can't go on unless Israel Spurlock is on hand to fling down his gun an' run when he hears a bung-shell playin' a tune in the air."

Captain Moseley coughed to hide a smile.

"It's jest like I tell you, Cap'in. The news is that we had a terrible victory at Chattanooga, but I notice in the Atlanta papers that the Yankees ain't no further north than they was before the fight; an' what makes it wuss, they are warmin' themselves in Chattanooga, whilst we are shiverin' outside. I reckon if Israel Spurlock had been on hand at the right time an' in the right place, we'd drove the Yanks plumb back to Nashville. Lord! I hope we'll have him on the skirmish line the next time we surround the enemy an' drive him into a town as big as Chattanooga."

Private Chadwick kept up his complaints for some time, but they failed to disturb the serenity of the captain, who urged his horse forward through the mist, closely followed by his companion. They finally left the valley, passed over the foothills, and began the ascent of Sugar Mountain. Here their journey became less disagreeable. The road, winding and twisting around the mountain, had been cut through a dense growth of trees, and these proved to be something of a shelter. Moreover, the road sometimes brought the mountain between the travelers and the wind, and these were such comfortable intervals that Mr. Chadwick ceased his complaints and rode along good-humoredly.

The two horsemen had gone about a mile, measuring the mountain road, though they were not more than a quarter of a mile from the foot, when they came suddenly on an old man sitting in a sheltered place by the side of the road. They came on the stranger so suddenly that their horses betrayed alarm, and it was all they could do to keep the animals from slipping and rolling into the gorge at their left. The old man was dressed in a suit of gray jeans, and wore a wool hat, which, although it showed the signs of constant use, had somehow managed to retain its original shape. His head was large and covered with a profusion of iron-gray hair, which was neatly combed. His face was round, but the lines of character obliterated all suggestions of chubbiness. The full beard that he wore failed to hide the evidences of firmness and determination; but around his mouth a serene smile lingered, and humor sparkled in his small brown eyes.

"Howdy, boys, howdy!" he exclaimed. "Tired as they look to be, you er straddlin' right peart creeturs. A flirt or two more an' they'd 'a' flung you down the hill, an' 'a' follered along atter you, headstall an' stirrup. They done like they weren't expectin' company in an' around here."

The sonorous voice and deliberate utterance of the old man bespoke his calling. He was evidently a minister of the gospel. This gave a clue to Captain Moseley's memory.

"This must be Uncle Billy Powers," said the captain. "I've heard you preach many a time when I was a boy."

"That's my name," said Uncle Billy; "an' in my feeble way I've been a-preachin' the Word as it was given to me forty year, lackin' one. Ef I ever saw you, the circumstance has slipped from me."

"My name is Moseley," said the captain.

"I useter know Jeremiah Moseley in my younger days," said Uncle Billy, gazing reflectively at the piece of pine bark he was whittling. "Yes, yes! I knowed Brother Moseley well. He was a God-fearin' man."

"He was my father," said the captain.

"Well, well, well!" exclaimed Uncle Billy, in a tone that seemed to combine reflection with astonishment. "Jerry Moseley's son! I disremember the day when Brother Moseley come into my mind, an' yit, now that I hear his name bandied about up here on the hill, it carries me plumb back to ole times. He weren't much of a preacher on his own hook, but let 'im foller along for to clench the sermon, an' his match couldn't be foun' in them days. Yit, Jerry was a man of peace, an' here's his son a-gwine about with guns an' pistols, an' what not, a-tryin' to give peaceable folks a smell of war."

"Oh, no!" said Captain Moseley, laughing; "we are just hunting up some old acquaintances. Some friends of ours we'd like to see."

"Well," said Uncle Billy, sinking his knife deep into the soft pine bark, "it's bad weather for a frolic, an' it ain't much better for a straightout, eve'y-day call. Speshually up here on the hill, where the ground is so wet and slipperyfied. It looks like you've come a mighty long ways for to pay a friendly call. An' yit," the old man continued, looking up at the captain with a smile that well became his patriarchal face, "thar ain't a cabin on the hill whar you won't be more than welcome. Yes, sir; wheresomever you find a h'a'thstone, thar you'll find a place to rest."

"So I have heard," said the captain. "But maybe you can cut our journey short. We have a message for Israel Spurlock."

Immediately Captain Moseley knew that the placid and kindly face of Uncle Billy Powers had led him into making a mistake. He knew that he had mentioned Israel Spurlock's name to the wrong man at the wrong time. There was a scarcely perceptible frown on Uncle Billy's face as he raised it from his piece of pine bark, which was now assuming the shape of a horseman's pistol, and he looked at the captain through half-closed eyelids.

"Come, now," he exclaimed, "ain't Israel Spurlock in the war? Didn't a posse ketch 'im down yander in Jasper an' take an' cornscrip' 'im into the army? Run it over in your mind now! Ain't Israel Spurlock crippled some'r's, an' ain't your message for his poor ole mammy?"

"No, no," said the captain, laughing, and trying to hide his inward irritation.

"Not so?" exclaimed Uncle Billy. "Well, sir, you must be shore an' set me right when I go wrong; but I'll tell you right pine blank, I've had Israel Spurlock in my min' off an' on ev'ry since they run him down an' kotch him an' drug 'im off to war. He was weakly like from the time he was a boy, an' when I heard you call forth his name, I allowed to myself, says I, 'Israel Spurlock is sick, an' they've come atter his ole mammy to go an' nuss him.' That's the idee that riz up in my min'."

A man less shrewd than Captain Moseley would have been deceived by the bland simplicity of Uncle Billy's tone.

"No," said he; "Spurlock is not sick. He is a sounder man than I am. He was conscripted in Jasper and carried to Adairsville, and after he got used to the camp he concluded that he would come home and tell his folk good-by."

"Now that's jes like Israel," said Uncle Billy, closing his eyes and compressing his lips —"jes like him for the world. He knowed that he was drug off right spang at the time he wanted to be getherin' in his crops, an' savin' his ruffage, an' one thing an' another beca'se his ole mammy didn't have a soul to help her but 'im. I reckon he's been a-housin' his corn an' sich like. The ole 'oman tuck on might'ly when Israel was snatched into the army."

"How far is it to shelter?" inquired Captain Moseley.

"Not so mighty fur," responded Uncle Billy, whittling the pine bark more cautiously. "Jes keep in the middle of the road an' you'll soon come to it. Ef I ain't thar before you, jes holler for Aunt Crissy an' tell her that you saw Uncle Billy some'r's in the woods an' he told you to wait for 'im."

With that Captain Moseley and Private

Chadwick spurred their horses up the mountain road, leaving Uncle Billy whittling.

"Well, dang my buttons!" exclaimed Chadwick, when they were out of hearing.

"What now?" asked the captain, turning in his saddle. Private Chadwick had stopped his horse and was looking back down the mountain as if he expected to be pursued.

"I wish I may die," he went on, giving his horse the rein, "if we haven't walked right square into it with our eyes wide open."

"Into what?" asked the captain, curtly.

"Into trouble," said Chadwick. "Oh," he exclaimed, looking at his companion seriously, "you may grin behind your beard, but you just wait till the fun begins—all the grins you can muster will be mighty dry grins. Why, Cap., I could read that old chap as if he was a newspaper. Whilst he was a-watchin' you I was a-watchin' him, an' if he ain't got a war map printed on his face I ain't never saw none in the *Charleston Mercury*."

"The old man is a preacher," said Captain Moseley in a tone that seemed to dispose of the matter.

"Well, the Lord help us!" exclaimed Chadwick. "In about the wuss whippin' I ever got was from a young feller that was preachin' an' courtin' in my neighborhood. I sorter sassed him about a gal he was flyin' around, an' he upped an' frailed me out, an' got the gal to boot."

"And have you been running from preachers ever since?"

"Not, as you may say, constantly a-runnin'," replied Chadwick; "yit I ain't been aflingin' no sass at 'em; an' my reason tells me for to give 'em the whole wedth of the big road when I meet 'em."

"Well," said the captain, "what will you do about this preacher?"

"A man in a corner is obleeged to do the best he kin. I'll jest keep my eye on him, an' the fust motion he makes, I'll—"

"Run?"

"Well, now," said Chadwick, "a man in a corner can't most ingener'lly run. Git me hemmed in, an' I'll scratch an' bite an' scuffle the best way I know how. It's human natur', an' I'm mighty glad it is; for if that old man's eyes didn't tell no lies we'll have to scratch

an' scuffle before we git away from this mountain."

Captain Moseley bit his mustache and smiled grimly as the tired horses toiled up the road. A vague idea of possible danger had crossed his mind while talking to Uncle Billy Powers, but he dismissed it at once as a matter of little importance to a soldier bent on carrying out his orders at all hazards.

It was not long before the two travelers found themselves on a plateau formed by a shoulder of the mountain. On this plateau were abundant signs of life. Cattle were grazing about among the trees, chickens were crowing, and in the distance could be heard the sound of a woman's voice singing. As they pressed forward along the level road they came in sight of a cabin, and the blue smoke curling from its short chimney was suggestive of hospitality. It was a comfortable-looking cabin, too, flanked by several outhouses. The buildings, in contrast with the majestic bulk of the mountain, that still rose precipitously skyward, were curiously small, but there was an air of more than ordinary neatness and coziness about them. And there were touches of feminine hands here and there that made an impression—rows of well-kept boxwood winding like a green serpent through the yard, and a privet hedge that gave promise of rare sweetness in the spring.

As the soldiers approached a dog barked, and then the singing ceased, and the figure of a young girl appeared in the doorway, only to disappear like a flash. This vision, vanishing with incredible swiftness, was succeeded by a more substantial one in the shape of a motherly looking woman, who stood gazing over her spectacles at the horsemen, apparently undecided whether to frown or to smile. The smile would have undoubtedly forced its way to the pleasant face in any event, for the years had fashioned many a pathway for it, but just then Uncle Billy Powers himself pushed the woman aside and made his appearance, laughing.

" 'Light, boys, 'light!" he exclaimed, walking nimbly to the gate. " 'Light whilst I off wi' your creeturs' gear. Ah!" he went on, as he busied himself unsaddling the horses, "you thought that while your Uncle Billy was amoonin' aroun' down the hill yander you'd steal a march on your Aunt Crissy, an' maybe come a-conscriptin' of her into the army. But not so—not so! Your Uncle Billy has been here long enough to get his hands an' his face rested."

"You must have been in a tremendous hurry," said Captain Moseley, remembering the weary length of mountain road he had climbed.

"Why, I could 'a' tuck a nap an' 'a' beat you," said the old man.

"Two miles of tough road, I should say," responded Moseley.

"Go straight through my hoss lot and let yourself down by a saplin' or two," said Uncle Billy, "an' it ain't more 'n a good quarter." Whereupon the old man laughed heartily.

"Jes leave the creeturs here," he went on. "John Jeems an' Fillmore will ten' to 'em whilst we go in an' see what your Aunt Crissy is gwine to give us for supper. You won't find the grub so mighty various, but there is plenty enough of what they is."

There was just enough of deference in Aunt Crissy's greeting to be pleasing, and her unfeigned manifestations of hospitality soon caused the guests to forget that they might possibly be regarded as intruders in that peaceful region. Then there were the two boys, John Jeems and Fillmore, both large enough and old enough, as Captain Moseley quietly observed to himself, to do military service, and both shy and awkward to a degree. And then there was Polly, a young woman grown, whose smiles all ran to blushes and dimples. Though she was grown, she had the ways of a girl—the vivacity of health and good humor, and the innocent shyness of a child of nature. Impulsive and demure by turns, her moods were whimsical and elusive and altogether delightful. Her beauty, which illumined the old cabin, was heightened by a certain quality that may be described as individuality. Her face and hands were browned by the sun, but in her cheeks the roses of youth and health played constantly. There is nothing more charming to the eye of man than the effects produced when modesty parts company with mere formality and conventionality. Polly, who was as shy as a ground squirrel and as grace-ful, never pestered herself about formalities. Innocence is not infrequently a very delightful form of boldness. It was so in the case of Polly Powers, at any rate.

The two rough soldiers, unused to the society of women, were far more awkward and constrained than the young woman, but they enjoyed the big fire and the comfortable supper none the less on that account. When, to employ Mrs. Powers's vernacular, "the things were put away," they brought forth their pipes; and they felt so contented that Captain Moseley reproved himself by suggesting that it might be well for them to proceed on their journey up the mountain. But their hosts refused to listen to such a proposal.

"Not so," exclaimed Uncle Billy; "by no means. Why, if you knowed this hill like we all, you'd hoot at the bar' idee of gwine further after nightfall. Besides," the old man went on, looking keenly at his daughter, "ten to one you won't find Spurlock."

Polly had been playing with her hair, which was caught in a single plait and tied with a bit of scarlet ribbon. When Spurlock's name was mentioned she used the plait as a whip, and struck herself impatiently in the hand with the glossy black thong, and then threw it behind her, where it hung dangling nearly to the floor.

"Now I tell you what, boys," said Uncle Billy, after a little pause; "I'd jes like to know who is at the bottom of this Spurlock business. You all may have took a notion that he's a no-'count sorter chap—an' he is kinder puny; but what does the army want with a puny man?"

"It's the law," said Captain Moseley, simply, perceiving that his mission was clearly understood. "He is old enough and strong enough to serve in the army. The law calls for him, and he'll have to go. The law wants him now worse than ever."

"Yes," said Private Chadwick, gazing into the glowing embers—"lots worse 'n ever."

"What's the matter along of him now?" inquired Mrs. Powers, knocking the ashes from her pipe against the chimney jamb.

"He's a deserter," said Chadwick.

"Tooby shore!" exclaimed Mrs. Powers. "An' what do they do wi' 'em, then?"

For answer Private Chadwick passed his right hand rapidly around his neck, caught hold of an imaginary rope, and looked upwards at the rafters, rolling his eyes and distorting his features as though he were strangling. It was a very effective pantomime. Uncle Billy shook his head and groaned, Aunt Crissy lifted her hands in horror, and then both looked at Polly. That young lady had risen from her chair and made a step towards Chadwick. Her eyes were blazing.

"You'll be hung long before Israel Spurlock," she cried, her voice thick with anger. Before another word had been said she swept from the room, leaving Chadwick sitting there with his mouth wide open.

"Don't let Polly pester you," said Uncle Billy, smiling a little at Chadwick's discomfiture. "She thinks the world an' all of Sister Spurlock, an' she's been a-knowin' Israel a mighty long time."

"Yes," said Aunt Crissy, with a sigh; "the poor child is hot-headed an' high-tempered. I reckon we've sp'ilt 'er. 'T ain't hard to spile a gal when you hain't got but one."

Before Chadwick could make reply a shrill, querulous voice was heard coming from the room into which Polly had gone. The girl had evidently aroused someone who was more than anxious to engage in a war of words.

"Lord A'mighty massy! whar's any peace?" the shrill voice exclaimed. "What chance on the top side of the yeth is a poor sick creetur got? Oh, what makes you come a-tromplin' on the floor like a drove of wild hosses, an' a-shakin' the clabberds on the roof? I know! I know!"—the voice here almost rose to a shriek, —"it's 'cause I'm sick an' weak, an' can't he'p myself. Lord! ef I but had strength!"

At this point Polly's voice broke in, but what she said could only be guessed by the noise in the next room.

"Well, what ef the house an' yard was full of 'em? Who's afeard? After Spurlock? Who keers? Hain't Spurlock got no friends on Sugar Mountain? Ef they are after Spurlock, ain't Spurlock got as good a right for to be after them? Oh, go 'way! Gals hain't got no sense. Go 'way! Go tell your pappy to come here an' he'p me in my cheer. Oh, go on!"

Polly had no need to go, however. Uncle Billy rose promptly and went into the next room.

"Hit's daddy," said Aunt Crissy, by way of explanation. "Lord! daddy used to be a mighty man in his young days, but he's that wasted wi' the palsy that he hain't more 'n a shadder of what he was. He's jes like a baby, an' he's mighty quar'lsome when the win' sets in from the east."

According to all symptoms the wind was at that moment setting terribly from the east. There was a sound of shuffling in the next room, and then Uncle Billy Powers came into the room, bearing in his stalwart arms a big rocking-chair containing a little old man whose body and limbs were shriveled and shrunken. Only his head, which seemed to be abnormally large, had escaped the ravages of whatever disease had seized him. His eyes were bright as a bird's, and his forehead was noble in its proportions.

"Gentlemen," said Uncle Billy, "this here is Colonel Dick Watson. He used to be a big politicianer in his day an' time. He's my father-in-law."

Uncle Billy seemed to be wonderfully proud of his connection with Colonel Watson. As for the colonel, he eyed the strangers closely, forgetting, apparently, to respond to their salutation.

"I reckon you think it's mighty fine, thish 'ere business er gwine ter war whar they hain't nobody but peaceable folks," exclaimed the colonel, his shrill, metallic voice being in curious contrast to his emaciated figure.

"Daddy!" said Mrs. Powers in a warning tone.

"Lord A'mighty! don't pester me, Crissy Jane. Hain't I done seed war before? When I was in the legislatur' didn't the boys rig up an' march away to Mexico? But you know yourself," the colonel went on, turning to Uncle Billy's guests, "that this hain't Mexico, an' that they hain't no war gwine on on this 'ere hill. You know that mighty well."

"But there's a tolerable big one going on over yonder," said Captain Moseley, with a sweep of his hand to the westward.

"Now, you don't say!" exclaimed Colonel Watson, sarcastically. "A big war goin' on an' you all quiled up here before the fire, out 'n sight an' out 'n hearin'! Well, well, well!"

"We are here on business," said Captain Moseley, gently.

"Tooby shore!" said the colonel, with a sinister screech that was intended to simulate laughter. "You took the words out 'n my mouth. I was in-about ready to say it when you upped an' said it yourself. War gwine on over yander an' you all up here on business. Crissy Jane," remarked the colonel in a different tone, "come here an' wipe my face an' see ef I'm a-sweatin'. Ef I'm a-sweatin', hit's the fust time since Sadday before last."

Mrs. Powers mopped her father's face, and assured him that she felt symptoms of perspiration.

"Oh, yes!" continued the colonel. "Business here an' war yander. I hear tell that you er after Israel Spurlock. Lord A'mighty above us! What er you after Israel for? All the fightin' he can do is to fight for his ole mammy."

Captain Moseley endeavored to explain to Colonel Watson why his duty made it imperatively necessary to carry Spurlock back to the conscript camp, but in the midst of it all the old man cried out:

"Oh, I know who sent you!"

"Who?" the captain said.

"Nobody but Wesley Lovejoy!"

Captain Moseley made no response, but gazed into the fire. Chadwick, on the other hand, when Lovejoy's name was mentioned, slapped himself on the leg, and straightened himself up with the air of a man who has made an interesting discovery.

"Come, now," Colonel Watson insisted, "hain't it so? Didn't Wesley Lovejoy send you?"

"Well," said Moseley, "a man named Lovejoy is on Colonel Waring's staff, and he gave me my orders."

At this the old man fairly shrieked with laughter, and so sinister was its emphasis that the two soldiers felt the cold chills creeping up their backs.

"What is the matter with Lovejoy?" It was Chadwick who spoke.

"Oh, wait!" cried Colonel Watson, "you may'nt want to wait, but you'll have to. I may look like I'm mighty puny, an' I speck I am, but I hain't dead yit. Lord A'mighty, no! Not by a long shot!"

There was a pause here, during which Aunt Crissy remarked in a helpless sort of way:

"I wonder wher' Polly is, an' what she's a-doin'?"

"Don't pester 'long of Polly," snapped the paralytic. "She knows what she's a-doin'."

"About this Wesley Lovejoy," said Captain Moseley, turning to the old man: "you seem to know him well."

"You hear that, William!" exclaimed Colonel Watson. "He asts me ef I know Wes Lovejoy! Do I know him? Why, the triflin' houn'! I've knowed him ev'ry sence he was big enough to rob a henroos'."

Uncle Billy Powers, in his genial way, tried to change the current of conversation, and he finally succeeded, but it was evident that Adjutant Lovejoy had one enemy, if not several, in that household. Such was the feeling for Spurlock and contempt for Wesley Lovejoy that Captain Moseley and Private Chadwick felt themselves to be interlopers, and they once more suggested the necessity of pursuing their journey. This suggestion seemed to amuse the paralytic, who laughed loudly.

"Lord A'mighty!" he exclaimed, "I know how you feel, an' I don't blame you for feelin' so; but don't you go up the mountain this night. Thes stay right whar you is, beca'se ef you don't you'll make all your friends feel bad for you. Don't ast me how, don't ast me why. Come an' put me to bed, William, an' don't let these folks go out'n the house this night."

Uncle Billy carried the old man into the next room, tucked him away in his bed, and then came back. Conversation lagged to such an extent that Aunt Crissy once more felt moved to inquire about Polly. Uncle Billy responded with a sweeping gesture of his right hand, which might mean much or little. To the two Confederates it meant nothing, but to Aunt Crissy it said that Polly had gone up the mountain in the rain and cold. Involuntarily the woman shuddered and drew nearer the fire.

It was in fact a venturesome journey that Polly had undertaken. Hardened as she was to the weather, familiar as she was with the footpaths that led up and down and around the face of the mountain, her heart rose in her

41

mouth when she found herself fairly on the way to Israel Spurlock's house. The darkness was almost overwhelming in its intensity. As Uncle Billy Powers remarked, while showing the two Confederates to their bed in the "shed-room," there "was a solid chunk of it from one eend of creation to t' other." The rain, falling steadily but not heavily, was bitterly cold, and it was made more uncomfortable by the wind, which rose and fell with a muffled roar, like the sigh of some Titanic spirit flying hither and yonder in the wild recesses of the sky. Bold as she was, the girl was appalled by the invisible contention that seemed to be going on in the elements above her, and more than once she paused, ready to flee, as best she could, back to the light and warmth she had left behind; but the gesture of Chadwick, with its cruel significance, would recur to her, and then, clenching her teeth, she would press blindly on. She was carrying a message of life and freedom to Israel Spurlock.

With the rain dripping from her hair and her skirts, her face and hands benumbed with cold, but with every nerve strung to the highest tension and every faculty alert to meet whatever danger might present itself, Polly struggled up the mountain path, feeling her way as best she could, and pulling herself along by the aid of the friendly saplings and the overhanging trees.

After a while—and it seemed a long while to Polly, contending with the fierce forces of the night and beset by a thousand doubts and fears—she could hear Spurlock's dogs barking. What if the two soldiers, suspecting her mission, had mounted their horses and outstripped her? She had no time to remember the difficulties of the mountain road, nor did she know that she had been on her journey not more than half an hour. She was too excited either to reason or to calculate. Gathering her skirts in her hands as she rose to the level of the clearing, Polly rushed across it towards the little cabin, tore open the frail little gate, and flung herself against the door with a force that shook the house.

Old Mrs. Spurlock was spinning, while Israel carded the rolls for her. The noise that Polly made against the door startled them both. The thread broke in Mrs. Spurlock's hand, and one part of it curled itself on the end of the broach with a buzz that whirled it into a fantastically tangled mass. The cards dropped from Israel's hands with a clatter that added to his mother's excitement.

"Did anybody ever hear the beat of that?" she exclaimed. "Run, Iserl, an' see what it is that's a-tryin' to tear the roof off'n the house."

Israel did not need to be told, nor did Mrs. Spurlock wait for him to go. They reached the door together, and when Israel threw it open they saw Polly Powers standing there, pale, trembling, and dripping.

"Polly!" cried Israel, taking her by the arm.

"In the name er the Lord!" exclaimed Mrs. Spurlock, "wher' 'd you drop from? You look more like a drownded ghost than you does like folks. Come right in here an' dry yourse'f. What in the name of mercy brung you out in sech weather? Who's dead or a-dyin'? Why, look at the gal!" Mrs. Spurlock went on in a louder tone, seeing that Polly stood staring at them with wide-open eyes, her face as pale as death.

"Have they come?" gasped Polly.

"Listen at 'er, Iserl! I b'lieve in my soul she's done gone an' run ravin' deestracted. Shake 'er, Iserl; shake 'er."

For answer Polly dropped forward into Mrs. Spurlock's arms, all wet as she was, and there fell to crying in a way that was quite alarming to Israel, who was not familiar with feminine peculiarities. Mrs. Spurlock soothed Polly as she would have soothed a baby, and half carried half led her to the fireplace. Israel, who was standing around embarrassed and perplexed, was driven out of the room, and soon Polly was decked out in dry clothes. These "duds," as Mrs. Spurlock called them, were ill-fitting and ungraceful, but in Israel's eyes the girl was just as beautiful as ever. She was even more beautiful when, fully recovered from her excitement, she told with sparkling eyes and heightened color the story she had to tell.

Mrs. Spurlock listened with the keenest interest, and with many an exclamation of indignation, while Israel heard it with undisguised admiration for the girl. He seemed to enjoy the whole proceeding, and when Polly in the ardor and excitement of her narration betrayed an almost passionate interest in his probable fate, he rubbed his hands slowly together and laughed softly to himself.

"An' jest to think," exclaimed Polly, when she had finished her story, "that that there good for nothin' Wesley Lovejoy had the imperdence to ast me to have him no longer'n last year, an' he's been a-flyin' round me constant."

"I seed him a-droppin' his wing," said Israel, laughing. "I reckon that's the reason he's after me so hot. But never you mind, mammy; you look after the gal that's gwine to be your daughter-in-law, an' I'll look after your son."

"Go off, you goose!" cried Polly, blushing and smiling. "Ef they hang you, whose daughter-in-law will I be then?"

"The Lord knows!" exclaimed Israel, with mock seriousness. "They tell me Lovejoy is an orphan!"

"You must be crazy," cried Polly, indignantly. "I hope you don't think I'd marry that creetur. I wouldn't look at him if he was the last man. You better be thinkin' about your goozle."

"It's ketchin' befo' hangin'," said Israel.

"They've mighty nigh got you now," said Polly. Just then a hickory nut dropped on the roof of the house, and the noise caused the girl to start up with an exclamation of terror.

"You thought they had me then," said Israel, as he rose and stood before the fire, rubbing his hands together, and seeming to enjoy most keenly the warm interest the girl manifested in his welfare.

"Oh, I wisht you'd cut an' run," pleaded Polly, covering her face with her hands; "they'll be here therreckly."

Israel was not a bad-looking fellow as he stood before the fire laughing. He was a very agreeable variation of the mountain type. He was angular, but neither stoop-shouldered nor cadaverous. He was awkward in his manners, but very gracefully fashioned.

After a while he became thoughtful. "I jest tell you what," he said, kicking the chunks vigorously, and sending little sparks of fire skipping and cracking about the room. "This business puzzles me—I jest tell you it does. That Wes Lovejoy done like he was the best

friend I had. He was constantly huntin' me up in camp, an' when I told him I would like to come home an' git mammy's crop in, he jest laughed an' said he didn't reckon I'd be missed much, an' now he's a-houndin' me down. What has the man got agin me?"

Polly knew, but she didn't say. Mrs. Spurlock suspected, but she made no effort to enlighten Israel. Polly knew that Lovejoy was animated by blind jealousy, and her instinct taught her that a jealous man is usually a dangerous one. Taking advantage of one of the privileges of her sex, she had at one time carried on a tremendous flirtation with Lovejoy. She had intended to amuse herself simply, but she had kindled fires she was powerless to quench. Lovejoy had taken her seriously, and she knew well enough that he regarded Israel Spurlock as a rival. She had reason to suspect, too, that Lovejoy had pointed out Israel to the conscript officers, and that the same influence was controlling and directing the pursuit now going on.

Under the circumstances, her concern—her alarm, indeed—was natural. She and Israel had been sweethearts for years—real sure-enough sweethearts, as she expressed it to her grandfather—and they were to be married in a short while; just as soon, in fact, as the necessary preliminaries of clothes making and cake baking could be disposed of. She thought nothing of her feat of climbing the mountain in the bitter cold and the overwhelming rain. She would have taken much larger risks than that; she would have faced any danger her mind could conceive of. And Israel appreciated it all; nay, he fairly gloated over it. He stood before the fire fairly hugging the fact to his bosom. His face glowed, and his whole attitude was one of exultation; and with it, shaping every gesture and movement, was a manifestation of fearlessness which was all the more impressive because it was unconscious.

This had a tendency to fret Polly, whose alarm for Israel's safety was genuine.

"Oh, I do wisht you'd go on," she cried; "them men 'll shorely ketch you ef you keep on a-stayin' here a-winkin' an' a-gwine on makin' monkey motions."

"Shoo!" exclaimed Israel. "Ef the house

was surrounded by forty thousan' of 'em, I'd git by 'em, an', ef need be, take you wi' me."

While they were talking the dogs began to bark. At the first sound Polly rose from her chair with her arms outstretched, but fell back pale and trembling. Israel had disappeared as if by magic, and Mrs. Spurlock was calmly lighting her pipe by filling it with hot embers. It was evidently a false alarm, for, after a while, Israel backed into the door and closed it again with comical alacrity.

"Sh-sh-sh!" he whispered, with a warning gesture, seeing that Polly was about to protest. "Don't make no fuss. The dogs has been a-barkin' at sperits an' things. Jest keep right still."

He went noiselessly about the room, picking up first one thing and then another. Over one shoulder he flung a canteen and over the other a hunting horn. Into his coat pocket he thrust an old-fashioned powder flask. Meanwhile his mother was busy gathering together such articles as Israel might need. His rifle she placed by the door, and then filled a large homespun satchel with a supply of victuals—a baked fowl, a piece of smoked beef, and a big piece of light bread. These preparations were swiftly and silently made. When everything seemed to be ready for his departure Israel presented the appearance of a peddler.

"I'm goin' up to the Rock," he said, by way of explanation, "an' light the fire. Maybe the boys 'll see it, an' maybe they won't. Leastways they're mighty apt to smell the smoke."

Then, without further farewell, he closed the door and stepped out into the darkness, leaving the two women sitting by the hearth. They sat there for hours, gazing into the fire and scarcely speaking to each other. The curious reticence that seems to be developed and assiduously cultivated by the dwellers on the mountains took possession of them. The confidences and the sympathies they had in common were those of observations and experience, rather than the result of an interchange of views and opinions.

Towards morning the drizzling rain ceased, and the wind, changing its direction, sent the clouds flying to the east, whence they had come. About dawn, Private Chadwick, who

had slept most soundly, was aroused by the barking of the dogs, and got up to look after the horses. As he slipped quietly out of the house he saw a muffled figure crossing the yard.

"Halt!" he cried, giving the challenge of a sentinel. "Who goes there?"

"Nobody, ner nothin' that'll bite you, I reckon," was the somewhat snappish response. It was the voice of Polly. She was looking up and across the mountains to where a bright red glare was reflected on the scurrying clouds. The density of the atmosphere was such that the movements of the flames were photographed on the clouds, rising and falling, flaring and fading, as though the dread spirits of the storm were waving their terrible red banners from the mountain.

"What can that be?" asked Chadwick, after he had watched the singular spectacle a moment.

Polly laughed aloud, almost joyously. She knew it was Israel's beacon. She knew that these red reflections, waving over the farther spur of the mountain and over the valley that nestled so peacefully below, would summon half a hundred men and boys—the entire congregation of Antioch Church, where her father was in the habit of holding forth on the first Sunday of each month. She knew that Israel was safe, and the knowledge restored her good humor.

"What did you say it was?" Chadwick inquired again, his curiosity insisting on an explanation.

"It's jest a fire, I reckon," Polly calmly replied. "Ef it's a house burnin' down, it can't be holp. Water couldn't save it now."

Whereupon she pulled the shawl from over her head, tripped into the house, and went about preparing breakfast, singing merrily. Chadwick watched her as she passed and repassed from the rickety kitchen to the house, and when the light grew clearer he thought he saw on her face a look that he did not understand. It was indeed an inscrutable expression, and it would have puzzled a wiser man than Chadwick. He chopped some wood, brought some water, and made himself generally useful; but he received no thanks from Polly.

She ignored him as completely as if he had

never existed, and all this set the private to thinking. Now a man who reflects much usually thinks out a theory to fit everything that he fails to understand. Chadwick thought out his theory while the girl was preparing breakfast.

It was not long before the two soldiers were on their way up the mountain, nor was it long before Chadwick began to unfold his theory, and in doing so he managed to straighten it by putting together various little facts that occurred to him as he talked.

"I tell you what, Captain," he said, as soon as they were out of hearing; "that gal's a slick 'un. It's my belief that we are gwine on a fool's errand. 'Stead of gwine towards Spurlock, we're gwine right straight away from 'im. When that gal made her disappearance last night she went an' found Spurlock, an' ef he ain't a natchul born fool he tuck to the woods. Why, the shawl the gal had on her head this mornin' was soakin' wet. It weren't rainin', an' hadn't been for a right smart while. How come the shawl wet? They weren't but one way. It got wet by rubbin' agin the bushes an' the limbs er the trees."

This theory was plausible enough to impress itself on Captain Moseley. "What is to be done, then?" he asked.

"Well, the Lord knows what ought to be done," said Chadwick; "but I reckon the best plan is to sorter scatter out an' skirmish aroun' a little bit. We'd better divide our army. You go up the mountain an' git Spurlock, if he's up thar, an' let me take my stan' on the ridge yander an' keep my eye on Uncle Billy's back yard an' hoss lot. If Spurlock is r'ally tuck to the woods, he'll be mighty apt to be slinkin' 'roun' whar the gal is."

Captain Moseley assented to this plan, and proceeded to put it in execution as soon as he and Chadwick were a safe distance from Uncle Billy Powers's house. Chadwick, dismounting, led his horse along a cow path that ran at right angles to the main road, and was soon lost to sight, while the captain rode forward on his mission.

Of the two, as it turned out, the captain had much the more comfortable experience. He reached the Spurlock house in the course of three-quarters of an hour.

In response to his halloo Mrs. Spurlock came to the door.

"I was a-spinnin' away for dear life," she remarked, brushing her gray hair from her face, "when all of a sudden I hearn a fuss, an' I 'lows ter myself, says I, 'I'll be boun' that's someone a-hailin',' says I; an' then I dropped ever'thin' an' run ter the door, an' shore enough it was. Won't you 'light an' come in?" she inquired with ready hospitality. Her tone was polite, almost obsequious.

"Is Mr. Israel Spurlock at home?" the captain asked.

"Not, as you might say, adzackly at home, but I reckon in reason it won't be long before he draps in. He hain't had his breakfas' yit, though hit's been a-waitin' for him tell hit's stone col'. The cows broke out last night, an' he went off a-huntin' of 'em time it was light good."

"I'll ride on," said the captain. "Maybe I'll meet him coming back. Good-by."

It was an uneventful ride, but Captain Moseley noted one curious fact. He had not proceeded far when he met two men riding down the mountain. Each carried a rifle flung across his saddle in front of him. They responded gravely to the captain's salutation.

"Have you seen Israel Spurlock this morning?" he asked.

"No, sir, I hain't saw him," answered one. The other shook his head. Then they rode on down the mountain.

A little farther on Captain Moseley met four men. These were walking, but each was armed—three with rifles, and one with a shotgun. They had not seen Spurlock. At intervals he met more than a dozen—some riding and some walking, but all armed. At last he met two that presented something of a contrast to the others. They were armed, it is true; but they were laughing and singing as they went along the road, and while they had not seen Spurlock with their own eyes, as they said, they knew he must be farther up the mountain, for they had heard of him as they came along.

Riding and winding around upward, Captain Moseley presently saw a queer-looking little chap coming towards him. The little man had a gray beard, and as he walked he had a movement like a camel. Like a camel, too, he had a great hump on his back. His legs were as long as any man's, but his whole body seemed to be contracted in his hump. He was very spry, too, moving along as active as a boy, and there was an elfish expression on his face such as one sees in old picture-books —a cunning, leering expression, which yet had for its basis the element of humor. The little man carried a rifle longer than himself, which he flourished about with surprising ease and dexterity—practising apparently some new and peculiar manual.

"Have you seen Israel Spurlock?" inquired Captain Moseley, reining in his horse.

"Yes! Oh, yes! Goodness gracious, yes!" replied the little man, grinning good-naturedly.

"Where is he now?" asked the captain.

"All about. Yes! All around! Gracious, yes!" responded the little man, with a sweeping gesture that took in the whole mountain. Then he seemed to be searching eagerly in the road for something. Suddenly pausing, he exclaimed: "Here's his track right now! Oh, yes! Right fresh, too! Goodness, yes!"

"Where are you going?" Moseley asked, smiling at the antics of the little man, their nimbleness being out of all proportion to his deformity.

For answer the little man whirled his rifle over his hump and under his arm, and caught it as it went flying into the air. Then he held it at a "ready," imitating the noise of the lock with his mouth, took aim and made believe to fire, all with indescribable swiftness and precision. Captain Moseley rode on his way laughing; but, laugh as he would, he could not put out of his mind the queer impression the little man had made on him, nor could he rid himself of a feeling of uneasiness. Taking little notice of the landmarks that ordinarily attract the notice of the traveler in a strange country, he suddenly found himself riding along a level stretch of tableland. The transformation was complete. The country roads seemed to cross and recross here, coming and going in every direction. He rode by a little house that stood alone in the level wood, and he rightly judged it to be a church. He drew rein and looked around him. Everything was unfamiliar. In the direction from which he supposed he had

come a precipice rose sheer from the table-land more than three hundred feet. At that moment he heard a shout, and looking up he beheld the hunchback flourishing his long rifle and cutting his queer capers.

The situation was so puzzling that Captain Moseley passed his hand over his eyes, as if to brush away a scene that confused his mind and obstructed his vision. He turned his horse and rode back the way he had come, but the way seemed to be so unfamiliar that he turned into another road, and in the course of a quarter of an hour he was compelled to acknowledge that he was lost. Everything appeared to be turned around, even the little church.

Meanwhile Private Chadwick was having an experience of his own. In parting from Captain Moseley he led his horse through the bushes, following for some distance a cow path. This semblance of a trail terminated in a blind path, and this Chadwick followed as best he could, picking his way cautiously and choosing ground over which his horse could follow. He had to be very careful. There were no leaves on the trees, and the undergrowth was hardly thick enough to conceal him from the keen eyes of the mountaineers. Finally he tied his horse in a thicket of blackjacks, where he had the whole of Uncle Billy Powers's little farm under his eye. His position was not an uncomfortable one. Sheltered from the wind, he had nothing to do but sit on a huge chestnut log and ruminate, and make a note of the comings and goings on Uncle Billy's premises.

Sitting thus, Chadwick fell to thinking; thinking, he fell into a doze. He caught himself nodding more than once, and upbraided himself bitterly. Still he nodded—he, a soldier on duty at his post. How long he slept he could not tell, but he suddenly awoke to find himself dragged backward from the log by strong hands. He would have made some resistance, for he was a fearless man at heart and a tough one to handle in a knockdown and drag-out tussle; but resistance was useless. He had been taken at a disadvantage, and before he could make a serious effort in his own behalf he was lying flat on his back with his hands tied and as helpless as an infant. He looked up and discovered that his captor was Israel Spurlock.

"Well, blame my scaly hide!" exclaimed Chadwick, making an involuntary effort to free his hands. "You're the identical man I'm a-huntin'."

"An' now you're sorry you went an' foun' me, I reckon," said Israel.

"Well, I ain't as glad as I 'lowed I'd be," said Chadwick. "Yit nuther am I so mighty sorry. One way or 'nother I knowed in reason I'd run up on you."

"You're mighty right," responded Israel, smiling not ill-naturedly. "You fell in my arms same as a gal in a honeymoon. Lemme lift you up." Thereupon Israel helped Chadwick to his feet.

"You ketched me that time, certain and shore," said the latter, looking at Spurlock and laughing; "they ain't no two ways about that. I was a-settin' on the log thar a-noddin' an' a-dreamin' 'bout Christmas. 'T ain't many days off, I reckon."

"Oh, yes!" exclaimed Spurlock, sarcastically; "a mighty purty dream, I bet a hoss. You was fixin' up for to cram me in Lovejoy's stockin'. A mighty nice present I'd 'a' been, tooby shore. Stidder hangin' up his stockin', Lovejoy was a-aimin' for to hang me up. Oh, yes! Christmas dreams is so mighty nice an' fine, I'm a great min' to set right down here an' have one er my own—one of them kin' er dreams what's got a forked tail an' fireworks mixed up on it."

"Well," said Chadwick, with some seriousness, "whose stockin' is you a-gwine to cram me in?"

"In whose else's but Danny Lemmons's? An' won't he holler an' take on? Why, I wouldn't miss seein' Danny Lemmons take on for a hat full er shinplasters. Dang my buttons ef I would!"

Chadwick looked at his captor with some curiosity. There was not a trace of ill-feeling or bad humor in Spurlock's tone, nor in his attitude. The situation was so queer that it was comical, and Chadwick laughed aloud as he thought about it. In this Spurlock heartily joined him, and the situation would have seemed doubly queer to a passer-by chancing along and observing captor and prisoner laughing and chatting so amiably together.

"Who, in the name of goodness, is Danny Lemmons?"

"Lord!" exclaimed Spurlock, lifting both hands, "don't ast me about Danny Lemmons. He's—he's—well, I tell you what, he's the bull er the woods, Danny Lemmons is; nuther more ner less. He hain't bigger 'n my two fists, an' he's 'flicted, an' he's all crippled up in his back, whar he had it broke when he was a baby, an' yit he's in-about the peartest man on the mountain, an' he's the toughest. An' more 'n that, he's got them things up here," Spurlock went on, tapping his head significantly. Chadwick understood this to mean that Lemmons, whatever might be his afflictions, had brains enough and to spare.

There was a pause in the conversation, and then Chadwick, looking at his bound wrists, which were beginning to chafe and swell, spoke up.

"What's your will wi' me?" he asked.

"Well," said Spurlock, rising to his feet, "I'm a-gwine to empty your gun, an' tote your pistol for you, an' invite you down to Uncle Billy's. Oh, you needn't worry," he went on, observing Chadwick's disturbed expression: "they're expectin' you. Polly's tol' 'em you'd likely come back."

"How did Polly know?" Chadwick inquired.

"Danny Lemmons tol' 'er."

"By George!" exclaimed Chadwick, "the woods is full of Danny Lemmons."

"Why, bless your heart," said Spurlock, "he swarms roun' here."

After Spurlock had taken the precaution to possess himself of Chadwick's arms and ammunition he cut the cords that bound his prisoner's hands, and the two went down the mountain, chatting as pleasantly and as sociably as two boon companions. Chadwick found no lack of hospitality at Uncle Billy Powers's house. His return was taken as a matter of course, and he was made welcome. Nevertheless, his entertainers betrayed a spirit of levity that might have irritated a person less self-contained.

"I see he's ketched you, Iserl," remarked Uncle Billy with a twinkle in his eye. "He 'lowed las' night as how he'd fetch you back wi' him."

"Yes," said Israel, "he thes crope up on me. It's mighty hard for to fool these army fellers."

Then and afterward the whole family pretended to regard Spurlock as Chadwick's prisoner. This was not a joke for the latter to relish, but it was evidently not intended to be offensive, and he could do no less than humor it. He accepted the situation philosophically. He even prepared himself to relish Captain Moseley's astonishment when he returned and discovered the true state of affairs. As the day wore away it occurred to Chadwick that the captain was in no hurry to return. Even Uncle Billy Powers grew uneasy.

"Now, I do hope an' trust he ain't gone an' lost his temper up thar in the woods," remarked Uncle Billy. "I hope it from the bottom of my heart. These here wars an' rumors of wars makes the folks mighty restless. They'll take resks now what they wouldn't dassent to of tuck before this here rippit begun, an' it's done got so now human life ain't wuth shucks. The boys up here ain't no better 'n the rest. They fly to pieces quicker 'n they ever did."

No trouble, however, had come to Captain Moseley. Though he was confused in his bearings, he was as serene and as unruffled as when training a company of raw conscripts in the art of war. After an unsuccessful attempt to find the road he gave his horse the rein, and that sensible animal, his instinct sharpened by remembrance of Uncle Billy Powers's corncrib and fodder, moved about at random until he found that he was really at liberty to go where he pleased, and then he turned short about, struck a little canter, and was soon going down the road by which he had come. The captain was as proud of this feat as if it were due to his own intelligence, and he patted the horse's neck in an approving way.

As Captain Moseley rode down the mountain, reflecting, it occurred to him that his expedition was taking a comical shape. He had gone marching up the hill, and now he came marching down again, and Israel Spurlock, so far as the captain knew, was as far from being a captive as ever—perhaps farther. Thinking it all over in a somewhat irritated frame of mind, Moseley remembered Lovejoy's eagerness to recapture Spurlock. He remembered, also, what he had heard the night before, and it was in no pleasant mood that he

thought it all over. It was such an insignificant, such a despicable affair, two men carrying out the jealous whim of a little militia politician.

"It is enough, by George!" exclaimed Captain Moseley aloud, "to make a sensible man sick."

"Lord, yes!" cried out a voice behind him. Looking around, he saw the hunchback following him. "That's what I tell 'em; goodness, yes!"

"Now, look here!" said Captain Moseley, reining in his horse, and speaking somewhat sharply. "Are you following me, or am I following you? I don't want to be dogged after in the bushes, much less in the big road."

"Ner me nuther," said the hunchback, in the cheerfulest manner. "An' then thar's Spurlock—Lord, yes; I hain't axt him about it, but I bet a hoss he don't like to be dogged atter nuther."

"My friend," said Captain Moseley, "you seem to have a quick tongue. What is your name?"

"Danny Lemmons," said the other. "Now don't say I look like I ought to be squeeze. Ever'body says that," he went on with a grimace, "but I've squeeze lots more than what's ever squeeze me. Lord, yes! Yes, siree! men an' gals tergether. You ax 'em, an' they'll tell you."

"Lemmons," said the captain, repeating the name slowly. "Well, you look it!"

"Boo!" cried Danny Lemmons, making a horrible grimace; "you don't know what you're a-talkin' about. The gals all 'low I'm mighty sweet. You ought to see me when I'm rigged out in my Sunday-go-to-meetin' duds. Polly Powers she 'lows I look snatchin'. Lord, yes! Yes, siree! I'm gwine down to Polly's house now."

Danny Lemmons walked on down the road ahead of the horse in the most unconcerned manner. It was part of Captain Moseley's plan to stop at Mrs. Spurlock's and inquire for Israel. This seemed to be a part of Danny's plan also, for he turned out of the main road and went ahead, followed by the captain. There were quite a number of men at Mrs. Spurlock's when Moseley rode up, and he noticed that all were armed. Some were standing listlessly about, leaning against the trees, some were sitting in various postures, and others were squatting around whittling; but all had their guns within easy reach. Mrs. Spurlock was walking about among them smoking her pipe. By the strained and awkward manner of the men as they returned his salutation, or by some subtle instinct he could not explain, Captain Moseley knew that these men were waiting for him, and that he was their prisoner. The very atmosphere seemed to proclaim the fact. Under his very eyes Danny Lemmons changed from a grinning buffoon into a quiet, self-contained man trained to the habit of command. Recognizing the situation, the old soldier made the most of it by retaining his good humor.

"Well, boys," he said, flinging a leg over the pommel of his saddle, "I hope you are not tired waiting for me." The men exchanged glances in a curious, shame-faced sort of way.

"No," said one; "we was a-settin' here talkin' 'bout ol' times. We 'lowed maybe you'd sorter git tangled up on the hill thar, and so Danny Lemmons, he harked back for to keep a' eye on you."

There was no disposition on the part of this quiet group of men to be clamorous or boastful. There was a certain shyness in their attitude, as of men willing to apologize for what might seem to be unnecessary rudeness.

"I'll tell you what," said Danny Lemmons, "they ain't a man on the mounting that's got a blessed thing agin you, ner agin the tother feller, an' they hain't a man anywheres aroun' here that's a-gwine to pester you. We never brung you whar you is; but now that you're here we're a-gwine to whirl in an' ast you to stay over an' take Christmas wi' us, sech ez we'll have. Lord, yes! a nice time we'll have, ef I ain't forgot how to finger the fiddle-strings. We're sorter in a quanderry," Danny Lemmons continued, observing Captain Moseley toying nervously with the handle of his pistol. "We don't know whether you're a-gwine to be worried enough to start a row, or whether you're a-gwine to work up trouble."

Meanwhile Danny had brought his long rifle into a position where it could be used promptly and effectually. For answer Moseley dismounted from his horse, unbuckled his belt

and flung it across his saddle, and prepared to light his pipe.

"Now, then," said Danny Lemmons, "make yourself at home."

Nothing could have been friendlier than the attitude of the mountain men, nor freer than their talk. Captain Moseley learned that Danny Lemmons was acting under the orders of Colonel Dick Watson, the virile paralytic; that he and Chadwick were to be held prisoners in the hope that Adjutant Lovejoy would come in search of them—in which event there would be developments of a most interesting character.

So Danny Lemmons said, and so it turned out; for one day while Moseley and Chadwick were sitting on the sunny side of Uncle Billy's house, listening to the shrill, snarling tones of Colonel Watson, they heard a shout from the roadside, and behold, there was Danny Lemmons and his little band escorting Lovejoy and a small squad of forlorn-looking militia. Lovejoy was securely bound to his horse, and it may well be supposed that he did not cut an imposing figure. Yet he was undaunted. He was captured, but not conquered. His eyes never lost their boldness, nor his tongue its bitterness. He was almost a match for Colonel Watson, who raved at all things through the tremulous and vindictive lips of disease. The colonel's temper was fitful, but Lovejoy's seemed to burn steadily. Moved by contempt rather than caution, he was economical of his words, listening to the shrill invective of the colonel patiently, but with a curious flicker of his thin lips that caused Danny Lemmons to study him intently. It was Danny who discovered that Lovejoy's eyes never wandered in Polly's direction, nor settled on her, nor seemed to perceive that she was in existence, though she was flitting about constantly on the aimless little errands that keep a conscientious housekeeper busy.

Lovejoy was captured one morning and Christmas fell the next, and it was a memorable Christmas to all concerned. After breakfast Uncle Billy Powers produced his Bible and preached a little sermon—a sermon that was not the less meaty and sincere, not the less wise and powerful, because the English was ungrammatical and the rhetoric uncouth. After it was over the old man cleared his throat and remarked:

"Brethren, we're gethered here for to praise the Lord an' do his will. The quare times that's come on us has brung us face to face with much that is unseemly in life, an' likely to fret the sperit an' vex the understandin'. Yit the Almighty is with us, an' of us, an' among us; an', in accordance wi' the commands delivered in this Book, we're here to fortify two souls in the'r choice, an' to b'ar testimony to the Word that makes lawful marriage a sacrament."

With that, Uncle Billy, fumbling in his coat pockets, produced a marriage license, called Israel Spurlock and his daughter before him, and in simple fashion pronounced the words that made them man and wife.

The dinner that followed hard on the wedding was to the soldiers, who had been subsisting on the tough rations furnished by the Confederate commissaries, by all odds the chief event of the day. To them the resources of the Powers household were wonderful indeed. The shed-room, running the whole length of the house and kitchen, was utilized, and the dinner table, which was much too small to accommodate the guests, invited and uninvited, was supplemented by the inventive genius of Private William Chadwick, who, in the most unassuming manner, had taken control of the whole affair. He proved himself to be an invaluable aid, and his good humor gave a lightness and a zest to the occasion that would otherwise have been lacking.

Under his direction the tables were arranged and the dinner set, and when the politely impatient company were summoned they found awaiting them a meal substantial enough to remind them of the old days of peace and prosperity. It was a genuine Christmas dinner. In the center of the table was a large bowl of eggnog, and this was flanked and surrounded by a huge dish full of apple dumplings, a tremendous chicken pie, barbecued shote, barbecued mutton, a fat turkey, and all the various accompaniments of a country feast.

When Uncle Billy Powers had said an earnest and simple grace he gave his place at the head of the table to Colonel Watson, who had been brought in on his chair. Aunt Crissy gave Chadwick the seat of honor at the foot, and then the two old people announced that they were ready to wait on the company, with Mr. Chadwick to do the carving. If the private betrayed any embarrassment at all, he soon recovered from it.

"It ain't any use," he said, glancing down the table, "to call the roll. We're all here an' accounted for. The only man or woman that can't answer to their name is Danny Lemmons's little brown fiddle, an' I'll bet a sev'm-punce it'd skreak a little ef I tuck it out 'n the bag. But before we whirl in an' make a charge three deep, le' 's begin right. This is Christmas, and that bowl yander, with the eggnog in it, looks tired. Good as the dinner is, it's got to have a file leader. We'll start in with what looks the nighest like Christmas."

"Well," said Aunt Crissy, "I've been in sech a swivet all day I don't reely reckon the nog is wuth your while, but you'll ha' ter take it thes like you fin' it. Hit's sweetened wi' long sweet'nin', an' it'll ha' ter be dipped up wi' a gourd an' drunk out 'n cups."

"Lord bless you, ma'am," exclaimed Chadwick, "they won't be no questions axed ef it's got Christmas enough in it, an' I reckon it is, 'ca'se I poured it in myself, an' I can hol' up a jug as long as the nex' man."

Though it was sweetened with syrup, the eggnog was a success, for its strength could not be denied.

"Ef I hadn't 'a' been a prisoner of war, as you may say," remarked Chadwick, when the guests had fairly begun to discuss the dinner, "I'd 'a' got me a hunk of barbecue an' a dumplin' or two, an' a slice of that chicken pie there—I'd 'a' grabbed 'em up an' 'a' made off down the mountain. Why, I'll tell you what's the truth—I got a whiff of that barbecue by daylight, an', gentulmen, it fairly made me dribble at the mouth. Nex' to Uncle Billy there, I was the fust man at the pit."

"Yes, yes," said Uncle Billy, laughing, "that's so. An' you holp me a right smart. I'll say that."

"An' Spurlock, he got a whiff of it. Didn't you all notice, about the time he was gittin' married, how his mouth puckered up? Along towards the fust I thought he was fixin' to dip down an' give the bride a smack. But, bless you, he had barbecue on his min', an' the bride missed the buss."

"He didn't dare to buss me," exclaimed Polly, who was ministering to her grandfather. "Leastways not right out there before you-all."

"Please, ma'am, don't you be skeered of Iserl," said Chadwick. "I kin take a quarter of that shote an' tote him plumb back to camp."

"Now I don't like the looks er this," exclaimed Uncle Billy Powers, who had suddenly discovered that Lovejoy, sitting by the side of Danny Lemmons, was bound so that it was impossible for him to eat in any comfort. "Come, boys, this won't do. I don't want to remember the time when any livin' human bein' sot at my table on Christmas Day with his han's tied. Come, now!"

"Why, tooby shore!" exclaimed Aunt Crissy. "Turn the poor creetur loose."

"Try it!" cried Colonel Watson, in his shrill voice. "Jest try it!"

"Lord, no," said Danny Lemmons. "Look at his eyes! Look at 'em."

Lovejoy sat pale and unabashed, his eyes glittering like those of a snake. He had refused all offers of food, and seemed to be giving all his attention to Israel Spurlock.

"What does Moseley say?" asked Colonel Watson.

"Ah, he is your prisoner," said Moseley. "He never struck me as a dangerous man."

"Well," said Chadwick, "ef there's any doubt, jest take 'im out in the yard an' give 'im han'-roomance. Don't let 'im turn this table over, 'cause it'll be a long time before some of this company'll see the likes of it ag'in."

It was clear that Lovejoy had no friends, even among his comrades. It was clear, too, that this fact gave him no concern. He undoubtedly had more courage than his position seemed to demand. He sat glaring at Spurlock, and said never a word. Uncle Billy Powers looked at him, and gave a sigh that ended in a groan.

"Well, boys," said the old man, "this is my house, an' he's at my table. I reckon we better ontie 'im, an' let 'im git a mou'ful ter eat. 'T ain't nothin' but Christian-like."

"Don't you reckon he'd better eat at the second table?" inquired Chadwick. This naïve suggestion provoked laughter and restored good humor, and Colonel Watson consented that Lovejoy should be released. Danny Lemmons undertook this gracious task. He had released Lovejoy's right arm, and was releasing the left, having to use his teeth on one of the knots, when the prisoner seized a fork—a large horn-handle affair, with prongs an inch and a half long—and, as quick as a flash of lightning, brought it down on Danny Lemmons's back. To those who happened to be looking it seemed that the fork had been plunged into the very vitals of the hunchback.

The latter went down, dragging Lovejoy after him. There was a short, sharp struggle, a heavy thump or two, and then, before the company realized what had happened, Danny Lemmons rose to his feet laughing, leaving Lovejoy lying on the floor, more securely bound than ever.

"I reckon this fork'll have to be washed," said Danny, lifting the formidable-looking weapon from the floor.

There was more excitement after the struggle was over than there had been or could have been while it was going on. Chadwick insisted on examining Danny Lemmons's back.

"I've saw folks cut an' slashed an' stobbed before now," he explained, "an' they didn't know they was hurt tell they had done cooled off. They ain't no holes here an' they ain't no blood, but I could 'most take a right pine-blank oath that I seed 'im job that fork in your back."

"Tut, tut!" said Colonel Watson. "Do you s'pose I raised Danny Lemmons for the like of that?"

"Well," said Chadwick, resuming his seat and his dinner with unruffled nerves, temper, and appetite, "it beats the known worl'. It's the fust time I ever seed a man git down on the floor for to give the in-turn an' the under-cut, an' cut the pigeon-wing an' the double-shuffle, all before a cat could bat her eye. It looks to me that as peart a man as Lemmons there ought to be in the war."

"Ain't he in the war?" cried Colonel Watson, excitedly. "Ain't he forever and eternally in the war? Ain't he my bully bushwhacker?"

"On what side?" inquired Chadwick.

"The Union, the Union!" exclaimed the colonel, his voice rising into a scream.

"Well," said Chadwick, "ef you think you kin take the taste out 'n this barbecue with talk like that, you are mighty much mistaken."

After the wedding feast was over, Danny Lemmons seized on his fiddle and made music fine enough and lively enough to set the nimble feet of the mountaineers to dancing. So that, take it all in all, the Christmas of the conscript was as jolly as he could have expected it to be.

When the festivities were concluded there was a consultation between Colonel Watson and Danny Lemmons, and then Captain Moseley and his men were told that they were free to go.

"What about Lovejoy?" asked Moseley.

"Oh, bless you! he goes over the mountain," exclaimed Danny, with a grin. "Lord, yes! Right over the mountain."

"Now, I say no," said Polly, blushing. "Turn the man loose an' let him go."

There were protests from some of the mountaineers, but Polly finally had her way. Lovejoy was unbound and permitted to go with the others, who were escorted a piece of the way down the mountain by Spurlock and some of the others. When the mountaineers started back, and before they had got out of sight, Lovejoy seized a musket from one of his men and turned and ran a little way back. What he would have done will never be known, for before he could raise his gun a streak of fire shot forth into his face, and he fell and rolled to the side of the road. An instant later Danny Lemmons leaped from the bushes, flourishing his smoking rifle.

"You see 'im now!" he cried. "You see what he was atter! He'd better have gone over the mountain. Lord, yes! lots better."

Moseley looked at Chadwick.

"Damn him!" said the latter; "he's got what he's been a-huntin' for."

By this time the little squad of militiamen, demoralized by the incident, had fled down the mountain, and Moseley and his companion hurried after them.

CHRISTMAS HYMN

LONG time ago the dawn of day
　　Streamed through the low roof thatched and
　　　　torn,
Where in the straw-clad manger lay
　　The Christ Child of the Virgin born.

Through His atonement draw we nigh;
　　GREAT GOD OF BATTLES! unto Thee
We lift our feeble voices high,
　　Grasp Thou the sword of victory.

Let harsh oppression pass away,
　　And want and sin from off the earth,
And ever sacred be the day
　　That gave the blessed Savior birth.

Let black-winged pestilence disappear,
　　And war with all its horrors cease,
And may we in the tempest hear
　　The solemn voice of Christ say "Peace!"
　　　　　　　　　　　　—ANONYMOUS

SANTA CLAUS
IN WARTIME

SANTA CLAUS IN CAMP

SANTA CLAUS VISITS THE NEW YORK *HERALD* OFFICE

(Christmas Eve, 1864)

FEW CELEBRATED individuals have visited New York without appearing at the *Herald* office, either publicly or *incog*. Therefore we are not easily astonished at any visit, however unexpected; yet we were somewhat amazed at a personage who dropped in upon us a night or two ago.

Suddenly the outer door of the Editorial Department opened. The sleepy office boy sprang up from his desk and was instantly alert. In a moment the boy made his appearance, striving to look as if he had never been asleep in his life, and briskly announced that somebody wanted to see the editor. The hour was late; but the *Herald* office is always open and ready for news. Indeed, late visitors are rather the rule than the exception. It was with no expectation of anything unusual, therefore, that we said, "Show the gentleman in." Upon the word, swift as a flash, a mysterious stranger appeared before us.

The stranger had a queer, quaint, and remarkable aspect. A great fur cap of the richest and darkest sable covered his head. An immense greatcoat, trimmed with the same choice fur, reached to his knees. The fur collar of this coat was upturned to cover his face. Long top boots, lined and trimmed with fur, covered his feet. In his hand he carried a black valise. At first sight we surmised that he might be a messenger from the Emperor of Russia. But on the other hand, his black valise looked suspicious.

At the thought, an imaginary odor of phosphorus filled the room. Was there an infernal machine in that black valise? So prompt are the operations of the mind that but a second or two had elapsed before we had framed, weighed, and dismissed them all, and were courteously asking the stranger to state his business.

"Sir," said the stranger, "I have often heard of the *Herald*. Since its first issue I have read it regularly." Of course we bowed. "You must often have heard of me, sir," he continued,

"indeed, you have mentioned my name in your columns not infrequently and never unfavorably." Of course we bowed again.

"Now," resumed the stranger, "don't say you don't know me, because that would be absurd." Absurd as it was, honesty compelled us to say it as politely as possible.

"Why," continued our mysterious visitor in the oddest, shrillest, and merriest little voice, "why, you don't mean it—you can't mean it—it's all humbug!"

Humbug or not, we did mean it, and so repeated it more emphatically. This seemed to take the stranger quite aback; but in a moment he recovered his self-possession and proceeded. *"Dunder und blitzen,"* said he—and we give his exact words: "That's what it is to be a historical personage! You have heard of me; all the world has heard of me, and yet you don't recognize me. I can't believe it! I won't believe it! Look at me."

As he said this, the stranger with a quaint gesture pulled off his cap, threw down his valise (which did not explode), opened his coat, and stepped into the full glare of the gaslight.

We did look at him, but were no wiser than before. He seemed a little old man, short and stout, with the jolliest red face, a nose set with the carbuncles of generous living, snowy white hair, and tiny bright twinkling eyes full of benevolence and fun. Beneath his great coat he wore an old-fashioned jacket which opened at the throat to disclose an equally old-fashioned ruffle and was decorated at the buttonhole with a sprig of Christmas greens and a cluster of hollies.

"Look at me again," said he; and we looked again, while the gaslights winked at him in the most familiar style, and the coal fire sparkled and crackled as if to welcome him. "Bless you!" he cried, advancing towards us on a sudden, "if you can't remember me I'll introduce myself! My name is Santa Claus, Kriss Kringle, or St. Nicholas. How do you do?" And with this he held out his hand.

The reader can imagine the astonishment of a sane and practical man at having such an announcement made in so practical a place as a daily newspaper office and in this most practical and skeptical year of Our Lord. Certainly this was no dream. The *Herald* establishment is not a favorable locality for dreams. Santa Claus forsooth? If our visitor had declared himself to be Hendrik Hudson, tired of playing ninepins and waiting for another Rip Van Winkle among the Kaatskills and on a visit to New York to see the sights of the town, we might perhaps have believed him. But as for Santa Claus—impossible! Evidently this was some mad old gentleman who had escaped his keepers and was out on a masquerade. Still, while we were arguing thus, the gaslights kept on winking like mad, the flames of the coal fire leaped up and down in frantic sport, and our mysterious visitor stood holding out his little fat dimpled hand. We took it. The best way to deal with insane persons is to humor them, and so we took the offered hand and shook it heartily.

But despite this concession, our face must have expressed our want of faith and our bewilderment, for the stranger was immensely amused and made the room ring with the most rollicking laughter. "Ho! ho!" cried the little

man, "he don't believe me! He won't believe that I am myself! This is too good!" And with this our mysterious visitor threw himself upon a chair, the arms of which appeared to embrace him most affectionately. "Ha! ha!" he cried again, jumping up from his seat and stamping merrily about the room, "I have known him since he was so high—and he thinks me a lunatic!"

We seized the opportunity to observe that he had expressed our opinion perfectly; but at this he laughed louder than ever. "Ho! ho!" the little man shouted, holding his sides with glee while the tears rolled down his jolly face, "this is too much. Put away those papers, close your desk, draw your chair to the fire, and I'll convince you of my identity if you be a reasonable man, and I think you are." Flattered by the compliment, mindful of the best mode to treat madmen, and seeing no other course to pursue, we obeyed.

The room felt unusually cozy and cheerful as we were seated by our mysterious visitor in front of the grate, and the fire, which had been inclined to die out before his arrival, now blazed up brilliantly as if stirred by an invisible poker.

"Sir," said the little man, "I know that it is against the rules of the establishment, but may I smoke?" As we nodded assent, he drew an old, large meerschaum pipe from his pocket, filled it from an old-fashioned pouch, and (perhaps accidentally) a coal of fire flew from the grate and set the tobacco aglow. "Now," said the stranger, "we are quite comfortable, and I may begin."

And he did begin by blowing out an immense cloud of fragrant smoke. "See, sir," he continued, "the influence of popular superstitions. They infect even so practical a man as yourself." (Mutual bows.) "If I had come down this fireplace you would have believed me to be either Santa Claus or a chimney sweep. If you had caught me busy with your children's stockings in the dead of night, you would have thought me either Kriss Kringle or a burglar. If you had seen me riding over the chimney tops in my sleigh drawn by Prancer and Dancer and the rest of my reindeer, you would have imagined me to be either St. Nicholas or a passing cloud. But because I walk in at the door like anybody else, you take me for a madman! My dear sir, do you suppose that because I have lived several centuries I am blind to the progress of the age? You might have learned better from my toys which I change and improve every year because I am well aware that the children of the present day, who must have crying dolls and self-propelling locomotives to please them, would not be content with the rude wooden toys with which I delighted their great-grandfathers and grandmothers when they too were little folks. Are my toys to have all the modern improvements and not myself? The great wide chimneys and open fireplaces of olden times were navigable, so to speak; but how could a stout old chap like me get down this narrow chimney, for instance, or up through those little holes in the floor which you call registers? Sir, in the country I still use the chimneys sometimes, just for the sake of old recollections; but in the city you have no chimneys wide enough for me, and the hot air would stifle me if I tried to get down; and so I use the doors or the windows, whichever seems the more convenient. As for my sleigh, that is still necessary in some countries; but here the railroads enable me to travel faster. Why, bless you! some people believe that Santa Claus don't know what a railroad is, and yet there is the evidence to the contrary right under their eyes in the form of a toy train for children! It's just like those folks to try to talk me down as an old fogy and tell their children 'not to hang up their stockings—Pa will bring them something'—as if any 'Pa' alive could supply the place of the real Santa Claus." With some show of indignation our visitor now puffed his pipe profoundly.

Whether it was that the sincerity of the above remarks and the air of self-consciousness which pervaded them had convinced us of the identity of our visitor with the character he professed to represent, or whether there was something in the firelight which converted us, we are not certain; but he had scarcely concluded his opening observations before we found ourselves tacitly admitting that he was Santa Claus in sober earnest.

This is evident from the hasty notes which we then jotted down of the following conversation. It began by our asking if his modern mode of entering houses by the doors or windows did not expose him to detection by the children. "Not at all," he replied, "for the good children are all asleep." We then suggested that certain bad children might possibly lie awake on purpose to see him. "I never visit bad children," was his brief and shrewd reply. Satisfied upon this point, we ventured to inquire how he managed to select his toys so as to please all the little ones. "Just as you make a newspaper to please everyone—by attending to my business industriously," he answered.

We asked where he procured his toys. "From every country in the world," said the little man. We begged to know what his Christmas gifts cost. "Millions and millions of dollars," said our visitor, "and you can easily calculate that it must be so. Take rich and poor together, I estimate the sum at five dollars for every man in Christendom, and often that is too little." It naturally occurred to us that he must have a tremendous revenue, and upon our putting this thought into words, he replied, "So I have; more than a thousand petroleum princes combined. All the gold mines, the diamond mines, the silver mines, the coal mines, the lead mines, the oil mines, and the iron, tin and copper mines in the world pay tribute to me. Every form of industry is taxed by me once a year. Let a man escape every other sort of taxation; he cannot escape mine. What is more, few wish to escape it. No other tax is so willingly paid."

The pride with which he said this is indescribable. He wielded his pipe like a scepter and looked every inch a king. Noticing this, and anxious to draw him out still further, we spoke of the vast responsibilities of his position. "Yes, yes, you may well say that," he continued, "mine is a busy life. As soon as one Christmas is over I begin to prepare for the next. New children are constantly arriving, and some going away to Heaven, and some becoming young men and young women as the years roll round. Changes, you see, all the while so my gifts must be changed too. What will suit a child this year will not suit it next. Often I leave a boy with a top or a hobby horse, and find him next year with a cigar in his mouth; or I present a little girl with a rag baby, and the next year she is crying for diamond earrings and long skirts. Being a father, you know how much trouble it is to take care of one child. Think then of the infinite labor required to take care of all the children in the world. And that is what I have to do." The same pride in saying this, the same flourish of his pipe, and the same regal air.

"But, sir," continued Santa Claus after a brief pause and a few puffs of his pipe, "this is a labor of love. Bless the children! I love them all. Rich or poor, sick or well, they are always pleasant to me. In the sturdy little toddlers I see the fathers and mothers of future generations, and I thank Heaven that they are destined to come under my parental care. Talk of the trouble of providing for children! Sir, it is outweighed a thousand times by the pleasure. When my work is over, I stand and rub my hands with glee as I see the little ones dreaming of the joys of Christmas morning. The stockings are all filled, the Christmas trees have bloomed with various gifts, and the little heads resting peacefully upon their pillows are crowded with joyful anticipations. I love to see the children smiling in their sleep.

"I love to see them waking with the earliest dawn and clambering out of bed to see what Santa Claus has brought. Such great eyes at a wooden horse! Such silent admiration of a popgun! Such bursts of ringing laughter at a jack-in-the-box! Such boundless content as, lifted into bed again, they see all their new treasures spread out upon the coverlid! And then I love to watch them at play. How hard these little men and women work at their amusements. Their round plump legs seem never to tire of running backward and forward with a wagon or a tiny train of cars which has its depot under a chair. What equestrians they are, and how they ride their hobby horses to and fro over rough roads for immense distances to see some absent uncle or auntie! With what patience they play the same games over and over again—and never weary! With what generalship they marshal their toy troops into line—these miniature Grants and Shermans! Their drums, their rattles, and their tin trumpets, so odious to most ears, make sweetest music to mine. No *prima donna* sings

so deliciously as a little girl putting her doll to sleep.

"And then," continued Santa Claus—his face beaming like a sun, and the lights and the fire dancing more madly than ever—"and then I love to watch the idiosyncrasies of children. Here is one profoundly pondering over the astounding phenomenon of a toy dog that barks when he squeezes it. His sister, with a doll whose cry has an amazing resemblance to the little dog's bark, accepts the squeaking as quite natural and does not ponder at all. Another little fellow breaks his penny whistle to see where the sound comes from. This little girl forgets her candies in her maternal cares, while that one leaves all her dolls and lets her toy kitchen become terribly disordered to stuff herself with *bonbons*. Here is a stout little

chap who kicks his picture books into a corner to make room for his architectural designs. There is another who, forgetting all else, sits absorbed in the lamentable history of Cock Robin. Another is ciphering up the spots upon his dominoes, while his little brother finds no such fun as playing at ball. It is the world in little, my dear sir. But the best of it is," said Santa Claus, chuckling to himself, "they don't tire of my gifts. When school is out they come back to play again. They go to sleep with their toy wonders clasped in their little hands, and I have seen them die"—and here the twinkling eyes of Santa Claus were dim—"I have seen them die with their dear eyes turned to take a last look at some favorite plaything—the oldest and ugliest of the toys, you may be sure—as if they were sorrier to leave that than all the rest of the world."

After a silence of a few moments, we ventured to ask our visitor a few questions, to which we received the following replies:

"Sir," said Santa Claus, "it is, as you say, a source of regret to me that the children do not see me, although I sometimes think that they recognize me in their dreams. But many of the blessings of this life come to us from sources we never behold and, since it is so ordained, we must be content. You remark that my portraits do not do me justice. That must be true, or else I should not have been obliged to introduce myself to you. Still, as very few artists have ever seen me, I cannot wonder at their failures. Nevertheless, you must admit that several of them have hit my general appearance pretty correctly." There was a trifle of vanity in this—an unconscious pulling down of the waistcoat and stroking of the beard—but we affected not to notice.

"You ask, sir, if I am as busy as ever this year. Busier, sir, busier! There are so many soldiers' children to look after, and alas! so many orphans. To these I am unusually tender, and it is the duty of every man to assist me. Ah, the brave old Christmas times in the South are over until the war is over. The hearthstones there are desolate. Children who ought to be playing with popguns are shouldering real muskets in the rebel armies. Oh, sir, it would make your heart bleed if I could tell you of the scenes I have witnessed in Southern homes during the past four years. They were dreadful, dreadful. Merry old man as I am, it saddens me to think of them. I went South as long as I could. I kept green the memory of Santa Claus in their hearts for three martial years. But now I find myself shut out at every point, and this Christmas they must do without me. Let us hope," he added prayerfully, "that before another Christmas comes round there will be a reunited Union, a permanent peace, and a Santa Claus for the children.

"But, my good sir," continued our visitor changing his tone and manner, "the hour grows late, and, like Hamlet's ghost, I must away at cockcrow. Let us be practical; allow me to explain my business here."

In vain we remonstrated and begged him to continue his interesting remarks. In vain we assured him that we were not at all sleepy and were only too glad to listen to him. The little old gentleman had an imperative manner and a certain good-natured obstinacy withal, and he turned a deaf ear to our entreaties. Jumping up from his seat and bustling cheerily about the room, in less time than it takes us to tell of it he had cleared the office table of its multifarious books, papers, and pens. Then, lifting his black valise from the floor, he took his place behind the table like a conjurer, and motioned us to be seated in front of him like a conjurer's audience. "Now, sir," said Santa Claus, "you are not about to see anything very wonderful; but I want you to remember what you do see."

As he said these words, Santa Claus opened his valise, and drawing forth a great number of toys, pushed them rapidly across the table for our inspection. "These, sir," said he, "are of the usual kind; but they are just the things for children." There were balls and bats, stoves and spinning wheels, dolls and diapers, carts and cats, engines and cars, fiddles and farmyards, guns and gingerbread, houses and humming tops, jumping jacks and jacks-in-the-box, lambs and looking glasses, men and marbles, nodding figures and nutcrackers, omnibuses and ogres, prints and paints, rattles and rocking horses, swords and squirrels, trumpets and tamborines, unicorns and ewers, whips and walking sticks.

"Here are more of the same sort," said Santa Claus, giving the black valise a cunning shake; and in a second the table was again covered with arks and animals, building blocks and letter blocks, bows and arrows, companies of infantry and companies of cavalry, doll heads and doll bodies, drums and drumsticks, games in boxes, gold and silver beads, hoes and hoops, kaleidoscopes and menageries, maps and metamorphoses, magic lanterns and skates, sleighs and spades, stilts and stables, stores and tea sets, furniture and forts, and hundreds of other things which have maintained their popularity for years and may be found at any toy shop.

"Now, sir," said Santa Claus, brushing all these things into a corner, "I'll show you something new. A porter is said to have invented it in his idle moments; but you and I know who put the idea into his head." It was the figure of a little Negro boy dressed in plantation style, which was suspended over a vibrating board by a thin wire. "Look at this," cried Santa Claus, tapping the board with his finger and beginning to whistle a jig. In a moment the feet kept time to the tune. He beat the double shuffle. He was down on his knees and up again. He did the grapevine twist. Not Dan Bryant in all his glory could accomplish better dancing.

"Here is another of the same sort, called the gymnasts." Two figures, suspended over a smooth surface, wrestled with each other with a grace and a vigor never surpassed at the Olympian games or by the Hanlon Brothers. "Walking dolls," cried Santa Claus, setting them upon the table as he spoke, "and locomotives which wind up like a clock and propel themselves, and steamboats which do the same.

"Here is a neat thing, and cheap." It was a set of ninepins on a small table. You knock down the ninepins with a ball and set them up by pulling a string. "Here's a very perfect doll. Look at it," said Santa Claus. It was a doll that opened its eyes, said 'papa' and 'mamma,' and wore a waterfall. The waterfall made it look very fashionable and ridiculous. "Here is a good toy," continued Santa Claus. It was a magic wheel. Circular pieces of pasteboard placed upon an axis and turned before a mirror form dancing figures for your amusement.

"Ah," sighed Santa Claus, "it is not so easy as it seems to invent a novel and acceptable toy. Two or three a year are all I can depend upon.

"Now let us examine some books." Saying which, he quickly emptied a lot of woolly animals, cups and balls, battledores, skipping ropes, balloons, dominoes, towns, cities, bureaus, bedsteads, donkeys, roosters, railroad trains and mooing cows upon the floor, adding them to the miscellaneous heap already there.

Once more Santa Claus opened the black valise, which appeared as inexhaustible as the purse of Fortunatus or Heller's magic bottle. "Here," said he, "is a splendid Christmas gift. It is a subscription for the new magazine called *Our Young Folks,* issued by Ticknor and Fields. Judging by the first number, it will be the best periodical of the kind in the country. These *Rollo* Books and *Franconia* Stories are not new, but they are as yet unrivalled. Mayne Reid's stories are all good for boys. The *Popgun* Stories are really admirable. Their authoress understands children and writes to please them. She don't instruct them too much, and her morals point themselves. This is high praise—and there are the books. Here we have the *American Boy's Book of Games.* Look at the engravings! Here are *Aunt Fanny's Nightcap Stories*—all good. *Robinson Crusoe* and all the new Crusoes are indispensable for boys. Gulliver and Aesop go together. All Hans Andersen's works are capital for children. Oliver Optic's books can be recommended. He has two new stories ready: the *Soldier Boy* and the *Sailor Boy.* Ballantyne's splendid works should be read by everybody. Here are good old Sandford and Merton in new dresses. *Rummical Rhymes* and *Comical Rhymes* are new and funny juveniles. *Mother Goose's Melodies,* in a dozen different styles of binding you see, but as melodious as ever. Here is an edition on linen for the benefit of those children who try to secure knowledge by eating their books. Alphabets by the hundred, sir," cried Santa Claus, tossing them out. "Here is the newest design—an *Alphabet of Animals. Cock Robin* and the *Frog Who Would A-Wooing Go* are illustrated by Stephens, and well done, as you see. *Tom Thumb* and *Little Red Riding Hood* come out together, and the story of this little lady is freshly told in verse by Stoddard. Fairy tales innumerable are here; but Hans Andersen's are the best. Why, sir, that man is one of the dearest friends I have. He must have lived among the fairies, he knows their ways so well.

"And let me tell you, sir," said Santa Claus dropping the black valise from which the beautiful books and toys and games still kept pouring, "let me tell you that I pity the child who does not read such books, and I pity the father who denies them to his children. O, rare and marvellous volumes, more interesting than any of the novels of after life, more delightful than any of the other pleasures of childhood! Happy the boy who builds huts with Crusoe, slays monsters with the Giant Killer, and has Goody Two Shoes for a sweetheart! Happy the girl who knows Red Riding Hood like a sister and is sure that fairies dance upon the grass plot. Show me a man base enough to destroy these illusions," cried Santa Claus, hitting the table with his fist till the toys jumped up and down imploringly and the woolly dogs chased the timid dolls about, "and I'll show you a person not fit to be trusted with a sixpence and totally destitute of a heart."

For the life of us we could not avoid laughing at this sudden and ridiculous termination of what promised to be a most eloquent harangue. Without being in the least degree angry, Santa Claus joined in our merriment.

"Sir," he began, "it is time for me to go. I have detained you too long, and you know that I have only another day to distribute my gifts. I have called to see you because you, like myself, have the people under your care. I provide pleasures for the children, and through them I influence the hearts of men and women. You influence the minds of persons of every age and condition, and thus strive to benefit mankind. I visit the firesides but once a year. The *Herald* goes there every day. My responsibilities are great; so are yours. What I am saying to you will be spread before all the people of this country and many of the people of other countries within a few short days. That is a miracle, sir, which is equal to any that I can perform, and a power which I cannot excel. If you can make anybody love Christmas more dearly, and celebrate it more heartily, and cherish more deeply the lessons of benevolence it conveys, do so, and I shall thank you. Coming but once a year, Christmas binds all men together with a common faith and in a common brotherhood. If there be a heart which does not warm under its glow, that heart does not deserve to beat.

"Tell the people to remember the poor on that day. This great city in which, being its patron saint, I have a peculiar interest, has recently fed large and distant armies, and no man, woman or child within its bounds should be without a Christmas dinner this year. Teach your readers to be generous. Let no man hold out his hand for alms on Christmas Day and be refused. In your city are the sick and the afflicted. Bid your readers visit them. There be those who shiver with cold and suffer from hunger. Let them be relieved. Be sure Santa Claus is provided with the means to enter every orphan home and mission in this metropolis. In the streets I see children, ragged and forlorn, barefoot and chilled, who have no homes which I may visit and no hope of brighter days. Let your readers be my agent and make those children happy. You spend millions a year upon your soldiers; you give fortunes to your generals and your admirals; in public and private charities you have no rivals on this globe—see to it, then, that the few thousands needed to give poor children a dinner and a toy be not withheld this Christmas tide. Rich as I am, and strong as I am, I draw my wealth from generous hands, my strength from benevolent hearts. If they fail me, Santa Claus will be no more. May the day never come when I shall be forgotten; for then I shall know that the world is no longer worthy to exist. May the day never come when the gifts which pass between you in my name are those of the pocket only, unaccompanied by the sentiment which has made them doubly precious for so many hundreds of years. And now, good-by! A Merrie Christmas to you and to all."

Before we could answer a word Santa Claus had taken his black valise and was gone. We heard no footsteps on the stairs, no closing of the door, and saw no one pass out into the silent street. The books and toys upon the table and the notebook in our hand were the only evidences that he had really been with us. The gaslights settled into their steady flame. The fire in the grate fell smouldering into ashes. As we sat down to write out this full and true account of the visit of Santa Claus we could but sincerely echo his parting benediction: A MERRIE CHRISTMAS TO YOU AND TO ALL.

From The New York *Herald*, December 24, 1864.

SANTA CLAUS IN THE CONFEDERACY

BY MARY A. M'CRIMMON

'Twas colder than Zero one Christmas Eve
night,
When far off in Lapland, the great Northern
Light
In streams of wild beauty illumined the skies,
Like joy when it sparkles from innocent eyes.
Old Santa Claus, seeing the hour at hand
When children get sleepy all over the land,
Put eight tiny reindeer to one little sleigh,
And seizing a bundle, he started away—
Far over the mountain and over the snow,
As light as a feather and swift as a roe.

At last on our chimney he drew up his team,
And stole out as silent and soft as a dream,
Lest hearing his footsteps on top of the house,
The children, all sleeping "as snug as a mouse,"
Might wake up and catch him with pockets and
hat
Stuffed full of nice candy, and much more than
that—
Nuts, raisins and apples, and all sorts of toys—
Exactly the thing for the girls and the boys.
As light as a feather he came down the flue,
That seemed to grow wider to let him get
through;
And there in a corner, all ranged in a row,
Were four little stockings, as white as the snow.
He smiled when he saw them, and winked his
old eye,
But waited a moment, and then passed them
by,
To peep through the curtains of two little beds,
Where, wrapped in sweet slumber, lay four
little heads;
And he read in the faces of each little pair,
Who'd acted the wisest throughout the past
year.
If one had been naughty, and told a white fib—
Another got angry and tore up her bib—

If *he* had his parents neglected to mind,
Or *she* to her playmates been rude or unkind,
From them he'd have taken to give to the rest,
For Santa Claus always gives most to the best.

But these little fellows, it seems, had done well,
For how much he gave them I hardly can tell—
To one he gave candy, a drum and an apple;
Another a pony—a beautiful dapple—
Birds, baskets and dollies, with sweet flaxen
curls,
Fruits, flowers and ribbons, he left for the
girls—
If either was slighted, I cannot tell which,
For all received something—and no one a
switch.
"Good night, little darlings," old Santa then
said,
And shaking with laughter, he turned from the
bed,
And mounting the chimney, he started to go
Far over the mountain and over the snow.

This happened one Christmas. I'm sorry to
write,
Our ports were blockaded, and Santa, tonight,
Will hardly get down here; for if he should
start,
The Yankees would get him, unless he was
smart;
They beat all the men in creation to *run,*
And if they could get him, they'd think it
fine fun
To put him in prison, and steal the nice toys
He started to bring to our girls and our boys.
But try not to mind it—tell over your jokes—
Be gay and be cheerful, like other good folks;
For if you remember to be good and kind,
Old Santa next Christmas will bear it in mind.

From *The Southern Illustrated News.*

THE NIGHT
AFTER CHRISTMAS

Anonymous

'TWAS the night after Christmas, when all through the house
Every soul was abed, and as still as a mouse;
The stockings, so lately St. Nicholas's care,
Were emptied of all that was eatable there.
The Darlings had duly been tucked in their beds—
With very full stomachs, and pains in their heads.

I was dozing away in my new cotton cap,
And Nancy was rather far gone in a nap,
When out in the nurs'ry arose such a clatter,
I sprang from my sleep, crying—"What is the matter?"
I flew to each bedside—still half in a doze—
Tore open the curtains, and threw off the clothes;
While the light of the taper served clearly to show
The piteous plight of those objects below;
For what to the fond father's eyes should appear
But the little pale face of each sick little dear?
For each pet that had crammed itself full as a tick,
I knew in a moment now felt like Old Nick.

Their pulses were rapid, their breathings the same,
What their stomachs rejected I'll mention by name—
Now Turkey, now Stuffing, Plum Pudding, of course,
And Custards, and Crullers, and Cranberry sauce;
Before outraged nature, all went to the wall,
Yes—Lollypops, Flapdoodle, Dinner, and all;
Like pellets which urchins from popguns let fly,
Went figs, nuts and raisins, jam, jelly and pie,
Till each error of diet was brought to my view,
To the shame of Mamma and Santa Claus, too.

I turned from the sight, to my bedroom stepped back,
And brought out a phial marked "Pulv. Ipecac.,"
When my Nancy exclaimed—for their sufferings shocked her—
"Don't you think you had better, love, run for the Doctor?"
I ran and was scarcely back under my room,
When I heard the sharp clatter of old Jalap's hoof.
I might say that I hardly had turned myself round,
When the Doctor came into the room with a bound.
He was covered with mud from his head to his foot,
And the suit he had on was his very worst suit;
He had hardly had time to put *that* on his back,
And he looked like a Falstaff half fuddled with sack.
His eyes, how they twinkled! Had the Doctor got merry?

63

His cheeks looked like *Port* and his breath smelled of *Sherry*.
He hadn't been shaved for a fortnight or so,
And the beard on his chin wasn't white as the snow.
But inspecting their tongues in despite of their teeth,
And drawing his watch from his waistcoat beneath,
He felt of each pulse, saying—"Each little belly
Must get rid"—here he laughed—"of the rest of that jelly."
I gazed on each chubby, plump, sick little elf,
And groaned when he said so, in spite of myself;
But a wink of his eye when he physicked our Fred
Soon gave me to know I had nothing to dread.
He didn't prescribe, but went straightway to work
And dosed all the rest, gave his trousers a jerk,
And, adding directions while blowing his nose,
He buttoned his coat; from his chair he arose,
Then jumped in his gig, gave old Jalap a whistle,
And Jalap dashed off as if pricked by a thistle;
But the Doctor exclaimed, ere he drove out of sight,
"They'll be well by tomorrow—good night, Jones, good night!"

From *Godey's Lady's Book and Magazine,* December 1861.

CHRISTMAS AT HOME

YULETIDE DIVERSIONS

SKATING AT
CHRISTMAS TIME

"THE RED BALL IS UP!" The ponds and lakes of Central Park are frozen over, and joy reigns supreme among the skaters. After half a dozen disappointments caused by the fickle character of the weather, the clear waters have yielded themselves up to the icy influence of General Jack Frost, and the prospect is that they will continue subject to that frigid commander for a good spell.

The ice yesterday afternoon was in splendid condition, notwithstanding the heavy snowfall of the preceding day. Men had been set to work in such strong force, and worked with such good will the moment the snow ceased falling, that the large pond was found to be in beautiful condition shortly after noon. Here and there were little mounds and ridges of hardened snow, but generally speaking, the icy surface was as smooth as glass. Singularly enough, considering the splendid opportunity, the attendance of skaters was by no means large. Only about five thousand people, at the highest estimate, were to be seen on the pond at any given moment; but the sport was relished all the better owing to that very circumstance by those whose enterprise and passionate love of the amusement prompted them to encounter the intensely cold gale for the purpose of enjoying the first day's skating in the Park. The slim attendance is to be explained, in some measure at least, by the fact that the familiar signal—the red ball—was not displayed on the railroad cars, contrary to the custom observed during the skating season for the last few winters.

Men, women, and children made up the assemblage of skaters, and the sliding continued up to a late hour without the occurrence of a single accident of any note whatever. The arrangements established by the Park Commissioners are about the same as last year, and the few changes observable are much for the better. The skates are lent out on cheaper rates, ditto sliding chairs, and refreshments may be had at reasonable rates at all the saloons licensed by the managers of the Park. Increased accommodations are afforded to persons who prefer to look on at the grand panorama of skating without participating in the sport themselves. Commodious buildings have been erected along the banks of the pond, and there a splendid view of the animating scene may be enjoyed with perfect comfort and security to the shins, skulls, and backs of those not on skates—an immunity which was not always certain before, when people without skates on their feet were obliged to venture on the ice if they desired to see the delightful amusement.

The furor for skating, which the opening of the Park ponds inaugurated some three or four years since, has not at all diminished. On the contrary, it would seem to be on the increase, judging from the extensive preparations which are in progress to meet the anticipated demand this season for facilities for a full enjoyment of the sport. This ice mania—if we may so term it—which has drawn all ages and sizes of Metropolitan humanity to trust themselves on the slippery surfaces of our little lakes and ponds, has developed the genius for combined action in an eminent degree. There is scarcely a skating pond within a radius of a dozen miles of the city which has not fallen into the hands of an association of some kind or another, having established rates of admission, and under as strict rules of management as at a theater or ballroom. The advantages of good order, decorum, and increased facilities for enjoyment follow as a matter of course, and hence the popularity of these combinations. Like other organizations for amusement, these associations announce their programs with as ostentatious a desire to cultivate popular patronage as the managers of our theaters or opera companies, and so long as an amusement so healthful, graceful and exhilarating, is not abused to an extent sufficient to lead to its abandonment by those whose presence is one of its chief attractions, just so long will the existing furor for the sport prevail. In order to prevent such abuse, skating associations should exclude all elements that will have any tendency to diminish the respectability of the recreation.

Skating and dancing are the only two forms of recreative exercise within the reach of the gentler sex, the former being infinitely more healthful than the latter, from the fact that the rapid motion through a clear, bracing atmosphere, incident to skating, quickens the circulation and introduces the pure oxygen of nature into the system, instead of the noxious gases of the ballroom, where the atmosphere is redolent of carbonic acid, frivolous tittle tattle, *eau de cologne,* insipid small talk, cutaneous exhalations, and simpering stupidity. The contrast, too, between the social surroundings of the skating pond and the ballroom is equally in favor of the outdoor recreation.

But there is one circumstance which tends to give skating the precedence over any other amusement, and that is the privilege a gentleman enjoys of imparting instruction in the art to his fair companion. To intervene, just in the critical moment, between her departure from the perpendicular and her assumption of the horizontal is to enjoy a combination of duty and pleasure not often within reach, and no relation is more calculated to produce tender attachments than that of pupil and tutor under such circumstances. In fact, the exercise not only brings roses to the cheeks, and imparts buoyancy to the spirits, but weaves nets to catch Cupid, and makes cages to retain him.

The sanitary benefits accruing from skating are great, and especially is the exercise advantageous to females. The prominent cause of the delicate and sickly constitutions of the majority of our city ladies arises from their great neglect of outdoor exercise and recreation. Two-thirds of their lives are passed in the artificial and poisonous atmospheres of their furnace-heated and poorly ventilated apartments. The result is that prevention of the exhalation of carbon and inhalation of oxygen which are of such vital importance to the health of every human being. The requisite action of the lungs in the expulsion of the death-dealing element of the air, generated by the operations of the system, and the reception of the life-giving properties of the atmosphere is never better promoted than while indulging in the vigorous exercise of skating. It is very necessary, however, that the lady be appropriately clad for the occasion, and special care paid to the avoidance of any sudden check to the perspiration induced by the exercise, as thereby the surface of the body is chilled, and the freely circulating blood is driven from the surface, where it properly belongs, to the vital portions of the system, the powers of which become overtaxed, and congestion or inflammation is generally the result. All the fatal colds induced by visits to the skating ponds are invariably the result of a carelessness of exposure easily avoidable—these drawbacks to the sport being alike peculiar to every other exercise whether indoors or out.

From The New York *Herald,* December 24, 1864.

CHRISTMAS AT UNDER-TOR

It was nearly three o'clock in the afternoon when, after the tedious winding through crowded New York streets, we sat in our sleigh on the Hoboken ferry boat. The ladies took the opportunity to settle their hoops and tuck their furs snugly about them. My reverend cousin, Stuyvesant, and I, on the driving seat, looked over the snow-crested wheelhouses at the gray, velvety surface of the river—the rugged Palisades edging it in brown outline above, and below a forest of frosted masts, puffing tugboats; the smooth, flat islands with their fortress crowns. The horses impatiently swung their necks, jingling in jerks the full strings of bells.

We were ashore, soon past the Elysian Fields, ice cream and oyster saloons, and the pretentious villas of Hoboken—all the country wrapped in snow. "Ger-lang, step out colts." Jingling with such evident merriment to the movement, the bells (I had taken care to secure plenty of them) brought appreciative curves of sympathy about every mouth. So plainly was it expressed as we instinctively glanced at one another, there was no need to speak it all at once—"How nice!"

Mrs. Grayson, Stuyvesant's wife, Cousin Daisy (a name she had won in infancy) we called her, asked, "When will we get to Under-Tor?"

"Between eight and nine, probably," I answered.

We sped on, chatting and laughing, and at one time Oscar Mare sang a beautiful little thing he called Hans Andersen's *Winter Song*.

At about half after four, the sun, ruddy after its December day's work, shone in patches through a bunch of low cedars in the west. Its red rays skimmed across the white spread fields—glistened in the frost drops on the bushes and trees, and flashed on the small windows of an old Dutch farmhouse on our right, as if they were plates of burnished metals. The three cows lowing in the barnyard had their red coats polished in the glow, and the fowls, seeking a roost on the boughs beneath the house eaves, cackled "good night" as the last streaks shot to them and disappeared. Some miles ahead appeared a part of the Tappan Zee. Above, streaks of gray clouds fleeced the fading sky.

It had been thawing for hours, but now, quickly, at the night's signal, it grew cold—cold and colder fast. A crust formed on the snow's surface, which the sleigh parted with a gentle crunching noise. Night settled fast, and now the roads in some places were entirely unbroken.

It was very dark, or would have been but for the snow. In that, the innumerable silver spangling above had its reflection. Otherwise there was only the occasional passing glimmer from a farmhouse. A dog here, and another miles off, gave melancholy mouth to the electric atmosphere. The wintry country night was bitterly cold, and magically undefined in starlight and snow. Behind, they talked and laughed, taking no account of time. At length I missed the road. That was not told to Stuyvesant until I was sure of having regained it. Notwithstanding furs and merriment, the cold made entrance, and growing discomfort found expression in embarrassing questions. At length, I had to confess that the roads had grown very heavy, and therefore the horses had to be humored; that we had missed the way; and finally, that it was eight o'clock, and those lights to the northeast were in Nyack. I did not know whether Upper or Lower Nyack; but we ought to have passed both two hours ago. The effects of my confession were dispiriting to the surprised and somewhat alarmed ladies.

On we went for another hour, our progress slower and slower; the horses tired; the roads worse; and I not sure of the direction. The full extent of the cold Stuyvesant and I felt, and we had to change the reins every few minutes. Behind, the fun had subsided, except Oscar's, who fed the drooping spirits with courageous witticisms and snatches of song; but the ladies muttered speculations and occasional complaints. Could it be possible?—as by the match with which Stuyvesant and I lighted our cigars, we saw my watch—ten o'clock!

"Stuyvesant," I whispered, "we are in for an adventure sure enough. I don't know exactly where we are, but the horses are about used up, and I'm frozen."

He turned and boldly told the party our

situation, trying to make it out as a jolly good joke. The ladies did not appreciate it, except little Lucy. She did not say much, but evidently thought it a most delightful experience of romantic reality. Adelaide and Mrs. Grayson were really alarmed, and I am pretty sure that as we drove on again, I heard Cousin Daisy repeating parts of Eastman's *Snow Storm:*

"But cold and dead by the sunken log,
Are they who came from the town."

We pushed on for another half hour, which seemed a whole night time, and then pulled up before a farmhouse, in which the inmates were a long while under blankets. A rascally cur screeched and yelped at us. That, however, and our united voices calling for about ten minutes, aroused someone, for we heard a sash frostily resist lifting, and a male nightmare full voice say, "What in the devil do you want?"

Stuyvesant asked for the necessary information, and we learned that we were twelve miles from our destination and four from the nearest village. The window dropped with a bang, but the word reached me, too, something like "jam," or "slam," or "ram."

On we struggled, with what expressions of comfort and cheer we could find for the ladies.

"Ho! Halloo!" sang out Stuyvesant in alarm, "where in the mischief are you driving, Earnest? Here we are over the runners in a drift."

The fact is, I had my eyes on a dark, irregular building just ahead, and I was trying to make out if it was a poorhouse or a jail. We had to get out of this position, however. "Gee-up—I tell you ger-lang," and I cut the horses with the whip. A jump and a crash! A whiffletree broken. A dainty little shrieked chorus, and there we were.

SCENE: Indistinct snowdrifts—a jagged fence —a dark, low, looming building. TIME: Eleven o'clock of a biting cold winter night. CHARACTERS: Three ladies and three gentlemen. Anxious to avoid the reproaches and consternation of my charge, I handed the reins to Stuyvesant, and jumping from the sleigh, started to make a reconnaissance of the cause of our

accident, which I hoped might also prove a shelter in our extremity. It was evidently not inhabited. The second story had been destroyed by fire. Charred boards and beams hung over the lower story. I tried the door, whose step was an immense millstone. I had to lift to open it, for it hung by one hinge. My matches quickly showed me the interior of a mill; wheels, belts, and grain bins; and I heard the stream, which had once urged it, rushing beneath. Another door opened into a medium-sized room which had apparently been used as a storeroom for grain, but which must have been originally intended for the miller's family, for there, to gladden my eyes, was a large open fireplace. Something more was necessary. I hurried out and went around the building. Piled against one side were several cords of wood, and there—and outhouse large enough to shelter my poor horses. I picked up the broken boards and splinters that lay in it, and then loading myself with sticks from the woodpile, hurried with them to that altar of our night's comfort—the great fireplace. The only paper I had was *Harper's Weekly,* and that with a Christmas sketch in it which I had preserved for my little niece. Nevertheless it must go. As I stooped to arrange the fire, I heard my disconsolate party calling from the sleigh. I answered by holding a match to the kindling. In a moment a red, sportive flame shot up. As I ran to the sleigh, I turned to see the windows of our ark illuminated in welcome.

Oscar's lame legs would serve him but poorly in the untrampled snow. As I wanted him to assist immediately to the mill, I bid him get on my back—in that way we had made many a Saturday's excursion in our boarding school days—and telling Stuyvesant to make up all the sleigh cushions and robes in bundles, and to get the ladies ready to move, I trotted off again to the mill. "Now, Oscar," said I, putting him down in the bright wood-lighted room, "keep that fire roaring. Stuyvesant will bring in wood enough: and above all things, strain your wit to keep the ladies up to brave good spirits."

Hardly had I finished speaking before Stuyvesant's brigade marched in. Ah! how their faces changed as they saw the crackling fire —snapping, fizzing, and blazing—throwing rays

AN OMNIBUS SLEIGH

and shadows on the heavy beams and joists overhead, and making silvery threads of many an ancient spider's home. Yes, the rosy cheeks and lips were now set off by smiles and eyes sparkling with appreciation of the comfortable scene. In a moment, with the quickness of feminine enthusiasm, they were turning boxes and barrels into seats, and voting the adventure "splendid." Stuyvesant had gone out for an armful of wood, and as I left them—for I had determined to take one of the horses and seek for a house where I might find provisions for both man and beast—six pretty feet were toasting before the fire, and Oscar's humor was finding a delighted audience. The most tired horse I unharnessed and put into the outhouse. On the other I started at a brisk trot up the cold dark road. When I had gone about three-quarters of a mile, I descried a light ahead. Yes, someone was up, for when somewhat nearer to the house, I saw the figure of a man walking up and down a room. He heard my approach,

too, and came to the door. I told him of our accident, and that I was in want of feed for my horses, and whatever I could get to make a meal or two for my party.

"Why, that's my mill, stranger, and you're welcome to its shelter. Got the old chimney going, too, eh? That's good. Oh, yes, I guess I can help you some. Come around to the barn and help yourself for the horses." He got a lantern, and when we reached the barn he gave me an immense bag to stow hay and feed in. And then my new acquaintance said, "Hitch your horse there and come in. The old woman has gone to bed, but I guess we can stir up something to eat." So he did: a couple of pumpkin pies, a loaf of bread, a saucer of butter, and a slice of cheese. These he packed in a basket, chatting with me all the while as if we were old friends, adding, at my suggestion, some plates, cups, knives, and steel forks. He promised to bring us a roast turkey and some coffee for breakfast.

71

It took me but a few minutes to get back to the mill. The horses were soon fixed for the night, and then I entered our hotel, where the laughter was sounding merrily. Two shawls, hung from the center beam, partitioned off a ladies' room. They were draped up now and showed couches of cushions and furs. An improvised plank table was the chief article of furniture in the gentlemen's apartments. The elegant starch box and barrel easy chairs and fauteuils were occupied about the fire. My arrival, loaded with provisions, was enthusiastically greeted. I had a bottle of whiskey in my valise. We prevailed upon the ladies to take some of that, warm, in place of the tea they missed, and now I very much doubt whether Very or Delmonico could furnish a meal that would be attended with more real good humor and merriment than that supper at midnight in the deserted mill.

After our jolly little meal the ladies dropped their wall, and we thereafter only heard their whispers. Our blankets were limited, but we could lie near the fire.

I woke in the morning to the sound of the mill stream flowing coldly beneath us, and to the trill of a sweet laugh behind the partition of shawls. Stuyvesant was out already; but Oscar lay coiled up in a second sleep, with the additional comfort of the robe our companion had deserted. I heard the outside door creaking, and hurried out. There stood my friend of last night, true to his promise, with a basket of eatables, and in one hand a tin wash basin and a kettle.

"A bright morning to you, sir. My old woman thought of several things your women folks might want," said our good samaritan, putting down his load. "And I have rigged up a new whiffletree for you. And I have seen, too, that your horses are fed."

I got my whiskey bottle and begged him to take a drop with me, which he did.

"Thank you, sir," said he, smacking his lips. "Thunder, that *is* good. Well, tomorrow is Christmas, so I wish you and your party a tremendous Merry Christmas."

In an hour we were stowed in the sleigh

GOING TO A PARTY IN WINTER.

again and on our way. Our mill owner thought that ten dollars greatly overpaid him for his trouble and contributions, but we forced it on him. The night's experience had not given a cold to any of the party. Indeed, the ladies seemed fresh and radiant—yes, as radiant as the young morning sun that silvered the whole country. Some little snow birds hopped along the fences and tweeted a low response to our sleigh bells. The scene was beautifully exhilarating, and the sleighing now grew excellent, so that in less than an hour we were climbing up the south side of the mountain range which sweeps down to the river, half a dozen miles north of Rockland Lake. And as we reached the top—how brilliant and inspiring was the picture below us! The frozen river, from the feet of the piled-up mountains near West Point, dotted here and there by a few skaters looking like ants on white sugar, the cedar-clothed land spears, piercing the river course now and then. A few more quickly traveled miles, and we were trotting up the avenue of Under-Tor. There, right before us was that architectural embodiment of hospitality—my Uncle Minot's house—large, cheerful, straggling and sheltering. Dear comfortable old Under-Tor! And hearing the singing, jingling bells, Colonel Minot, tall and erect, his silver hair blowing about his head, comes to the door, smiling affection and cordiality to bid us "Welcome to Under-Tor."

Christmas Eve was nearly ended. We waited silently to hear the distant village clock strike twelve. Grandmother asked Stuyvesant to read the record of that event which made the whole civilized world commemorate it in thankfulness and joy tonight. Lights were brought, and he read that first part of the second chapter of *Luke,* shutting the book as he concluded with those words of glorious beauty and everlasting import: "And suddenly there was with the angel a multitude of the heavenly host praising God, and saying, 'Glory to God in the highest, and on earth peace, good will toward men.'" And then we all sang with hearts and voices:

> "Hark! the herald angels sing
> Glory to the new born King."

—the village bells clanging out with our song their joyous peals and Christmas Eve was numbered with the happy hours past of the receding year.

We left grandmother, mother, and Colonel Minot in the library, and all ran in a burst of mirth to the dining room. What a racket, laughing and popping of champagne!

"Cousins, cousins," exclaimed Mr. Grayson, "do let's have tableaux and charades tomorrow night."

"Splendid idea," was the unanimous answer. "We will—we will." Christmas had begun as merrily as ever it did. Oscar, in a solemn voice, cried out: "I propose a serious toast, and I excuse all those who may have conscientious scruples from drinking it. It is a Merry Christmas to all!"

"Merry Christmas!" "Merry Christmas!" And the girls set to hugging and kissing one another as if this was their first meeting after years of separation. "Merry, Merry Christmas!"

A noisy, gay, busy house was that of Under-Tor on Christmas morning. The great hall was to be turned into a theater. Carpenters were erecting a stage at one end. What a combination of sounds—laughing, sawing, talking, hammering! Figures hurrying in and out, groups on the stairs and the floor; someone busy in some way everywhere; ladies preparing costumes; ladies stitching up the long widths of green baize for a curtain, ladies all busy and chatting together over piles of prints and illustrated papers; the "Dresden Gallery" on the floor; the "Vernon Gallery" open on a sofa. Over the "Costumes of Italy" Oscar—and what a guest to be valued was he—Oscar proposing and elucidating charade words in a circle of ladies, was almost bewildered by impossible suggestions, by assents and obstacles.

The program for the evening commenced with tableaux and charades; then dancing, and after that, supper. The preparations crowded the day with busy pleasure, and for the evening we expected any amount of jollity.

It seemed to me that Uncle's dogs kept up a tremendous barking that afternoon. About sunset, someone wanted Adelaide to take her place in a rehearsal of "Faust and Marguerite," the third tableau on the list. She could not be found. They searched the parlors

and libraries. Then I went upstairs and knocked at her room door. Not there. So I got a lady's maid to look in the different rooms, but she was not upstairs. I went down again and out on a side piazza, where I could see if she were tramping about anywhere in the trodden paths of the hillside. I was about to go in again, when I heard the shutting of a door—the door of a small brick wing where Uncle once had a sort of office. There I saw Adelaide turning the key in the lock. I ran up to her before she had got it in her pocket. Her face was radiant with pleasure, but it changed when she saw me. "Why, Adelaide, what is going on out here?"

"No matter, Earnest—I shall tell you nothing about it. Just be quiet; and promise me, dear Earnest, that you will not say one word about this." And she took my arm in the insinuating way sisters have when they are determined to make you yield. "Promise me, now—that you will not mention where you found me. Earnest, do you hear?"

At half after seven everything was arranged in our theater. Those actors who would soon be wanted had retired to their green rooms, and the audience came in. Besides the members of our household, all the servants included, there were guests invited from the village.

The theater bell was just ringing for the raising of the curtain, when the dogs commenced barking again. Then came a rapping at the main door of the hall. My uncle opened it. There stood a stooping old man, supporting himself with a cane. His hair and long beard were almost as white as the snow. A long cloak was wrapped about his figure. He re-

moved his hat and spoke to Colonel Minot in a hoarse, trembling voice.

"Good evening, sir. I am a stranger in the village, but hearing of the festivities here, I have made bold to ask that I may be a looker-on tonight."

"Certainly, my good man, we are happy to see you. Do walk in."

I was among the audience and watched with much interest the man, whose old limbs took him slowly to a seat against the wall beneath the shadow of the stairs.

The tableaux went off perfectly. The last, "Christmas," a picture Oscar suggested, was strikingly beautiful and as effective as the greatest hit at Wallack's. Then came charades; some of them full of wit. The audience shouted with laughter, and when they could not guess the words, called for a repetition.

During the charade before the last, I looked to see how our old gentleman was getting on, but he was nowhere to be seen. I had not time to ask questions or express surprise before I was called for the last charade. In the first syllable "Sur," I was required to be extremely pressing in my attentions to a very pretty bar maid, Lucy Estvan. She reproved and repulsed the attentions of the impolite young dandy with an energetic and constant use of "Sir! *Sir,* you astonish me! Sir, I shall not permit you flatteries." The following syllable, "prise," was added, when a press gang burst into the room and bore me off a prisoner. The bar maid's relief, and yet her pity for "the poor young fellow lugged off so suddenly to sea," were sweetly acted. The curtain fell, and for the whole word I was to appear again, a full-blown sailor, after a long absence, to the astonished eyes of my admired bar maid. I was soon ready when, greatly to my astonishment, Adelaide ran up with resistless impetuosity and, clapping a hand over my mouth, pushed me, before I was aware of what she was about, into the green room (a large closet with a window on a piazza), and turned the key on me. I jumped through the window and was in a moment at the hall door, suspecting some stage joke of Adelaide's. The curtain rolled up. Lucy was seen dusting the barroom. The stage door opened, and there entered—the old gentleman Uncle had admitted an hour ago to witness the performance. Lucy's stage manner was gone in an instant. She was evidently as much amazed as any of the audience. "Ah!" said the old cracked voice, bringing out the words slowly, "Ah—I thought—I would come up here—to—to wish you all—a merry—very Merry Christmas!" In the twinkling of an eye his figure straightened, the cloak was thrown back, the white wig and beard were thrown across the stage. A delighted shout from a score of voices spread excitedly, joyfully through the hall.

"Harry? Yes! Yes! it is Harry!" Lucy fainted and would have fallen, but that happy-faced robust, handsome sailor caught her in his arms and pressed a kiss to her forehead. Adelaide took her from him, and he sprang with one bound among the audience. My mother had advanced from her seat, tears of joy filling her eyes. In a moment the restored son was clasped to her bosom, kisses pressed on his bronzed features, and two thankful hearts beat close to one another. A few minutes, and then uncle, brothers, sisters, all surrounded Harry. Arms around his neck, hands squeezing his; kisses, sobs, laughter! The mother, whose joy forbade words, silently thanked her God for this blessed, blessed Christmas. And all felt beyond expression the overflowing happiness of that merry Christmas.

God grant that before the end of another year we may, North and South, enjoy in one great strong Union an honorable, endurable peace. Peace! Peace to restore the blessings now withheld; to soothe and comfort thousands of hearts now worn sore with watching and fears; peace to bring back to us the brave, noble hearts we love so dearly! Can we not catch a reflection from its beautiful white wings *now*, as with overflowing heart we say, *"A Merry, Merry Christmas to all"*?

Anonymous pamphlet, New York, 1864.

Courtesy W. E. West, Vice President and Treasurer of Nationwide Insurance Companies

CHRISTMAS SNOW — A CURRIER AND IVES PRINT

A RICHMOND GIRL GOES TO THE COUNTRY FOR CHRISTMAS

BY MRS. BURTON HARRISON
(Mrs. Harrison's husband was Jefferson
Davis' secretary.)

IT WAS EVIDENT to all older and graver people that the iron belt surrounding the Southern country was being gradually drawn closer and her vitality in mortal peril of exhaustion. Our armies were dwindling, those of the North increasing with every draft and the payment of liberal bounties. Starved, nearly bankrupt, thousands of our best soldiers killed in battle, their places filled by boys and old men, the Federal Government refusing to exchange prisoners; our exports useless because of armed ships closing in our ports all along the coast, our prospects were of the gloomiest, even though Lee had won victory for our banners in the East. We young ones, who knew nothing and refused to believe in "croakers," kept on with our valiant boasting about our invincible army and the like; but the end was beginning to be in sight.

Christmas in the Confederacy offered as a rule little suggestions of the festival known to plum-pudding and robin-red-breast stories in annuals. Every crumb of food better than the ordinary, every orange, apple, or banana, every drop of wine and cordial procurable, went straightway to the hospitals, public or private. Many of the residents had set aside at least one room of their stately old houses as a hospital, maintaining at their own expense as many sick or wounded soldiers as they could accommodate. On Christmas Eve, all the girls and women turned out in the streets, carrying baskets with sprigs of holly, luckily plentiful, since the woods around Richmond still held its ruddy glow in spots where bullets had not despoiled the trees beyond recall.

Our little household had been gladdened by the return of our midshipman from Charleston, where he had been again on duty, and his re-establishment on board the "Old Pat," as their schoolship was called by the youngsters. Just here opened a delightful vision. We were all invited to spend Christmas at "The Retreat," in King William County, the way being then open and without danger of interruption, save by overfull rivers. The postscript to this agreeable epistle was brief, but to the point: "Bring your own gentlemen!" After much merriment in deciding whom this would include, the matter settled down into finding out who could be got to go. Of the limited supply of men who could get off for the jaunt, our friends Lee Tucker, naval paymaster, Confederate States, and Captain Joseph Denègre, of the ordnance department, with my small brother, were happily found available, and in the gray dawn of a December morning we set off by train from Richmond. At the last minute it was discovered that Midshipman Cary had forgotten his passport, he and Mr. Tucker remaining behind to secure it, thus necessitating a walk next day of half the distance from the terminus of their railway journey, the rest of the way by a hired buggy.

At our stopping-place, reached about 9 A.M. after a cold and joggling run by train, finding Uncle Nebuchadnezzar in waiting in a covered wagon lined with straw, we inquired of him the distance to the house.

Evening found us still in the wagon, less buoyant than at the start. When, toward sunset, we finally turned in at the Retreat gate, amid the barking of dogs and the rush outdoors of our glad host and their children, attended by scarcely less welcoming Negroes, all woes were forgotten. Two minutes later we were in enjoyment of intense physical relief, seated around a fire of generous logs sending out a glow that wrapped us in its warmth; and in half an hour we sat down to a table heaped with old-time luxuries: partridges, a sugar-cured ham, spareribs, and sausage—for those who knew what pork at the Retreat could be—corn pone, biscuits, fresh, delicious butter, pitchers of mantling cream, and coffee, hot, rich, fragrant, *tasting* of the bean! We had literally no words!

Dear, cheery little "Cousin Nannie," our hostess, despairing because Nebuchadnezzar had taken the wrong ford, thereby causing our delay and suffering, did not stop lamenting over us till we had eaten a disgraceful amount of supper. As soon as possible, she insisted that we girls should go to our rooms, and there, sinking into lavender-scented, linen-spread featherbeds, with a fire dancing itself out upon the hearth, and a smiling Negro woman waiting to extinguish the candles, elysium was attained. Was it true—could such home comforts still be for us war-worn children of the Confederacy? The last sounds in my waking ears were the patter of childish feet upon the landing, and a merry little golden-haired elf putting her head in at the door to cry, "I'll catch you, Christmas gift!" Then the strong, delicious aroma of forest greens from the hall below was wafted in as someone in authority captured the tiny invader and bore her off—and so—oblivion!

Next day, a quiet, cosy morning on a sofa wheeled up before the fire, with winter sunbeams glancing through crimson curtains into a room bowered in Christmas garlands. At midday a ramble through a forest heavy with pine odors, where a carpet of brown needles and dry twigs crackled musically under foot, amid currents of warm perfumed air; across denuded fields, where morning rime still glittered in fence corners upon the skeletons of last summer's wild flowers, and in the wide blue sky overhead crows wheeled and cawed—peace everywhere, peace infinite, no evil sight or sound to break the spell; and best of all, on our return to the house to find our two lost sheep of yesterday arrived and safe in the fold! To have had our boy miss that dinner would have robbed it of all savor.

Such a dinner! Served at three o'clock P.M. (after a luncheon, at twelve, of cordials and cakes), the host at his end of the long table, dispensing an emperor among turkeys, "Cousin Nannie" at hers, engaged in carving another ham (that of the night before having already gone to its long rest among the house servants)—a ham befrilled with white paper, its pink slices cut thin as shavings, the fat having a nutty flavor—with cloves stuck into a crust of sugar. I remember a course of game, and then the plum pudding, with a berg of vanilla ice cream and a mould of calves'-foot jelly, together with many little iced cakes and rosy apples in pyramids. This for us who had been for months living on salt pork and rice, beans and dried apples, who were to live on that fare (and in short rations, too) until poor old Richmond fell! The deeds done with fork and spoon that day, are they not written in the annals of the Retreat?

Once more unto the breach, dear friends! Our holiday was over. Again packed in the wagon, this time with the warmth of kindly good-byes and the memory of a royal welcome forming a shield around our hearts against cold and all Pandora's box of ills. "And just look here!" said Joe Denègre as we started, designating a large split basket of luncheon hidden in the straw. "Then, don't any of you say there's such a word as trouble in this world!"

We creaked along. We sank into deep ruts and dragged through miry reaches. The drive seemed endless. The cork came out of our persimmon beer and it filled Lee Tucker's shoe, but nobody complained. The victim, possessing a very nice voice of his own, started: "If you want to have a good time, jine the cavalry," in which everybody chimed. Other songs followed, and catches: "Frère Jacques!" "A southerly wind and a cloudy sky," and "White sand and gray sand." At two o'clock we had luncheon, and a happy silence fell.

More songs; then "Muggins" was proposed. Next, Mr. Tucker got out *Elsie Venner,* and gave us an example of his elocution in the tea party of Mrs. Marilla Rowens, and so we arrived at a ford that of course we couldn't cross.

To crown all, it was raining. Captains Denègre and Tucker went off in the gathering darkness through mud ankle-deep, reappearing with news of a house somewhere into which we might be taken. Whatever failed us in those days, it was not Virginian hospitality! The good people whose home we invaded seemed more than pleased to receive us, and next morning betimes started us again "On to Richmond." By that time all Christmas cheer had gone out of us. To reach a ferry, where there was only a tiny makeshift of a skiff, we and the mules wearily took up the burden of life again, plodding five miles through sloughs of hopeless mud, up perpendicular hills and down again, till every bone ached and philosophy ceased to be a virtue.

Once more on the shores of classic Pamunkey, liquid mud flowing everywhere, in prospect a crossing, two by two, in a miserable egg-shell made of slimy planks, the bottom quite under water! The crowning feat of our expedition was, on reaching the other shore, all vehicles failing, to take heart of grace and walk six miles, in a downpour, to the nearest station of the railway. If it is asked what were our notions of perfection, I would answer that in those days we were sustained by what Cervantes styled "the bounding of the soul, the bursting of laughter, and the quicksilver of the five senses."

From *Recollections Grave and Gay* by Mrs. Burton Harrison. Scribners, New York, 1911.

CHRISTMAS IN THE CITY AND COUNTRY

CHRISTMAS, the general holiday, has its charms for each. In town there is much consultation as to toilet, for though the children absorb the morning, and it is proper to be seen at church, it is not less certain that the intimate gentleman friends of the family will make their appearance by the time a demi-toilet can be dispatched, a little rehearsal of the general reception that marks the New Year. There are symptoms of it in the well-spread lunch table of the luxurious drawing room, in the *impromptu* grouping of ladies of the house with the first tinkle of the doorbell, and its enjoy-

ment culminates in the entrance of "the coming man," who "takes the liberty of bringing his friend Marks," already well known in society as "superb in the German."

Their country cousins, meantime, have already dined!—unfashionable creatures—and enjoyed with keen appetites the ample bountiful Christmas dinner the barnyard and the garden's latest gifts of crisp celery, winter vegetables, and fruit have contributed to. The air is keen and clear, the sky unclouded sapphire, the roads in their prime of sleighing from yesterday's travel over the last cheerful snowstorm. They, too, have "gentlemen friends" who are only too happy to pay their *devoirs* in the clear open air, and in much merriment the sleighing party is made up to dash along with chiming bells and song and laughter. An upset now and then is counted in with the amusements of the day, so that no one is hurt, and who ever is? by a fall into a yielding snowbank!

We leave our lady friends to choose for themselves in which scene lies the best opportunity for amusement and—*a proposal!*

From *Godey's Lady's Book* for December 1860.

CHRISTMAS MORNING

CHRISTMAS TABLEAUX

DEAR SUSY: I must tell you that grandmother Moore is going to give a grand family party. All the children, grandchildren, aunts, cousins, from far and near, are to be invited to spend the day.

We had arranged that all the gifts were to be sent to grandmother's to be distributed. A week beforehand, grandma sent for Gracie and me, and gave us *carte blanche* for the evening's entertainments. We accordingly moved all our tableaux arrangements from home and fitted up grandma's back parlor. We decked the front parlor with evergreens, hollyberries, and everlastings, and over the folding doors which separate the rooms we made in green and crimson berries the words "A Merry Christmas."

The company, nearly forty in all, assembled to dine at four, and darkness came on before they left the table. Leaving them to chat over the nuts and wine, our party of performers stole away from the dining room to arrange our costumes, scenery, and other little matters. There was some little impatience amongst the younger ones, but grandmother contrived to keep them upstairs until at seven o'clock we gave the signal for them to assemble in the front parlor. Here we had arranged the seats in rows facing the back parlor, and as soon as all were comfortably seated, we lowered the gas till the room was almost wholly dark.

All being now ready, Aunt Bessie began to play a slow dream waltz, the piano being entirely concealed from the audience. Then the curtain rose very slowly to disclose the moving tableau of "A Visit from Saint Nicholas."

The scene was arranged for a bedroom. In the center of the background was a large square of black cambric to represent the open fireplace, and in front of this hung two stockings. In the center of the foreground was a trundle bed, with Minnie and Eddie fast asleep, and on a sofa to the left Harry in a dressing gown, slippers, and lounging cap, lay half awake. Morris, concealed, read the poetry—

" 'Twas the night before Christmas, and all through the house
Not a creature was stirring, not even a mouse," etc.,

to the line

"When out on the lawn there arose such a clatter
I sprang from my couch to see what was the matter."

Here Harry sprang up and looked out and, while Morris read the description of Kriss Kringle on the roof, he kept up a running accompaniment of jingling sleighbells and tramping reindeer till the lines:

"As I drew in my head, and was turning around,
Down the chimney St. Nicholas came with a bound,"

when Gracie darted from behind the black cambric patch. She had insisted upon having the part, and she looked irresistibly droll. Her tiny figure was padded until she was almost as broad as she was long. She wore a great coat of crimson, trimmed with fur, which fell from her shoulders to her feet; a long white beard, a white wig, and a tall fur cap altered her beyond recognition, and she carried a short pipe in her mouth. Upon her back was a large basket of toys, with which she filled the stockings, giving all the by-play of the verses while Morris read them. Then, laying her finger aside of her nose, she vanished behind the black cambric again. A whistle, jingle of sleighbells, and then she cried: "Happy Christmas to all, and to all a good night." And the curtain fell upon our first picture.

The second was Kriss Kringle's Call.

The scene was a parlor, where Aunt Harriet, Uncle Walter, Minnie, Eddie, little Charley Moore, Julia Hastings, and some other of the children cousins were grouped, reading, playing, or sewing; a quiet home circle.

AUNT HARRIET: Tomorrow is Christmas, and we must be ready for Kriss Kringle.

PREPARING FOR THE CHRISTMAS PARTY

UNCLE WALTER: In Germany the old gentleman makes it a practice to call on Christmas Eve upon the parents of all good children to inquire what the little ones prefer for presents.

JULIA: I wish it were the fashion here. I have often wanted to see our good friend of Christmas.

(A word of explanation here. Grandma Moore has an Irish girl, who was raised in some unknown region, for until last year she never heard of St. Nicholas.)

(A violent ringing at the bell).

UNCLE WALTER: Who can that be, at this hour?

(Enter Molly, her red hair greased till it shone like a mirror, her clean dress and tidy apron as smooth as hands could make them.)

MOLLY: Sure, sir, there's a gentleman at the door, askin' for yourself.

UNCLE WALTER: Who is he, Molly?

UNCLE WALTER: And he gave no name?

MOLLY: Never the whisper of a name, only took his pipe outen his mouth. It's the beautifulest white beard he's got, sir. And sez he,

"Is Mr.——" Och! there's himself entirely.

(Enter Walter, in full Kriss Kringle costume, with alum on his beard and fur to represent icicles.)

WALTER: You will excuse my haste, sir. I was in Germany some five minutes ago—

MOLLY: Did ever anybody hear the like of that for a lie?

WALTER: And, hearing your children express a wish to see me—

MOLLY: Och, hear 'em all the way to Germany!

WALTER: I came over for a short call.

AUNT HARRIET: You are most heartily welcome. Pray, take a seat near the fire.

WALTER: I must lose no time. Will you allow me, madam, to examine these children, and see if they have learned anything since last year?

AUNT HARRIET: Certainly.

WALTER: Minnie, you cannot spell very well, I hear. Now, spell me transatlantic telegraph, backwards.

MINNIE: Yes, sir. H-u-m-b-u-g-, humbug.

83

WALTER: Excellent! Choose from my pack. (Minnie draws out a big red apple, and retires to eat it.)

WALTER: Charley, who was the most successful king who ever reigned in France?

CHARLEY: Napoleon Second, for he never had a chance to reign, and so could not fail.

WALTER: Julia, from where do we export most flour?

JULIA: From Aunt Hettie's garden, sir; she don't have anything in it but flowers.

WALTER: Julia, here is one chestnut for you; be very careful not to make yourself sick with it.

JULIA: I'll try *nut,* sir. (The clock strikes twelve.)

WALTER: Dear me, how time flies! I ought to be half way to Holland before this. Stand clear, children. Good evening, madam and papa; I'll call again tomorrow.

Here the curtain fell, and we sent all the performers front, while Walter, Harvey, Gracie, and I prepared for the grand tableau of the evening.

Aunt Bessie played *Adeste Fideles,* and the curtain was slowly drawn up. The frame was gone, and the brown curtain had likewise vanished. In the center of the room stood a Christmas tree which reached from floor to ceiling and branched out on each side almost touching the walls. High up among the branches was our Gracie, in white floating dress, loose curls, and a long wand, the Christ Child of the evening. All the gifts were upon the tree, and much of our week's work was explained in the little labels which fluttered from each one. Every gift had an appropriate line or verse attached to it.

Gracie's wand had a hook on the end, and was long enough to reach every part of the tree. After all had been sufficiently admired, the distribution of gifts began. Walter stood under the tree and received the articles as Gracie unhooked them, then read aloud the verse attached, and passed them to Harvey or me, and we distributed them in the proper order.

If my letter gives you one suggestion for your own evening's entertainment, it will not have been written in vain. Lovingly,

ELLA

_____

From *Godey's Lady's Book,* December 1861.

ON FIRST SEEING THE CHRISTMAS TREE

A HOMEMADE CHRISTMAS

BY T. P. W.

"NO CHRISTMAS PRESENTS this year; every dollar must be saved for that unfortunate debt to Mr. T——."

"No Christmas presents this year!" It sounded sadly, and Auntie sat thinking what could be done. Yes, there were nieces, nephews, and other loved ones—what *can* be done? Now that they all know there can be no expensive presents, the simple gifts of olden time would have to be acceptable.

Auntie hurried downtown, and bought bristol board, gold paper, bright colored sewing silks, emery, white wax, colored worsteds, and bits of merino; the old patterns that forty years since gave variety to fairs were brought into requisition.

There were emery bags, and little wax fishes with golden scales and fins; there were needle-books of bristol board cut in points and wound with bright colored silks, and between the leaves of these little books dimes were curiously fastened. There were merino pin cushions, wrought with colored worsted; and baskets of bristol board cut like oak leaves, bound with gold paper, and pleasant verses written between the veins of the leaves. When Christmas Eve came, there were twenty-seven little packages in readiness for distribution, the whole amount of the cost being $2.85!

The servants received useful gifts on Christmas morning; the rest were reserved for the evening of Christmas Day, when the representatives of five families were to have a social gathering.

"You must all come and spend the evening with us," said Auntie, "but we can only have a very simple supper."

The extension table, drawn to its full extent in the back parlor, covered with a clean tablecloth and ornamented with flowers and evergreens, looked bright and cheery, and there was room for all the guests. Uncle Ellis asked a blessing, and then there was a moment's silence, for all were looking at Auntie. Close by the oyster tureen was an elegant silver soup ladle. On one side was engraved "H. D. Ellis"; on the other, "For Auntie, from Karl

and Ella." There were tears in Auntie's eyes, and she could only give the loved donors a look of affectionate gratitude.

The soup plates were not grouped by the tureen, but one turned down for each guest. In taking them up, Auntie's simple presents appeared, exciting as much apparent pleasure and eliciting as many notes of admiration as the most expensive jewelry could have done.

Never was there a more cheerful supper, or one more heartily enjoyed. When the meal was finished, the little ones were directed to amuse themselves in their own way. The whole house was thoroughly warmed and lighted, and every room opened. They bounded away in merry glee, with Uncle Frank as leader in all their sports and frolics.

The piano was opened, and, after many modern pieces and songs, Auntie was urged to play some old tunes. "Please play the first march you ever learned." "The Bugle March" was played, followed by "Auld Lang Syne" and "Adeste Fideles," with variations. Then we sang hymns, in which all joined.

At length the little ones came into the parlor thoroughly tired. It was strange, for the old family clock that had for seventy years been a perfect timepiece pointed only to nine. On looking at watches, it was found to be half past ten; there was much winking and laughing among the children, but no one would tell who persuaded the old clock to stop precisely at nine.

"Now we must hurry and get home as soon as possible."

"Before separating, let us unite in prayer."

We knelt while Uncle Ellis offered a fervent, heartfelt prayer. When we rose from our knees, there were a few moments of hushed silence, for all felt the presence of the Saviour, whose advent had this day been celebrated. After cloaks, overcoats, hoods, and furs were on, there was a reassembling in the parlor for last words.

"What a delightful evening!"

"I never enjoyed myself so well before!"

There was a general kissing of Uncle Ellis and Auntie, a cheerful "good night," and then the merry sleigh bells sounding in different directions told us that the loved ones were going to their homes.

From *Godey's Lady's Book* for December 1861.

SKETCH ON THE LARGE POND.

'GETTING READY.'

CENT[

REFRESHMENTS.

HOT COFFEE

W I

PUT YOUR SKATES ON, MISTER.

NEW YORK SKATING CLUB.

PARK

WARMING UP

BY THOMAS NAST

THE CHRISTMAS TREE

BY LIZZIE M'INTYRE

"OH, I wish it was tomorrow!" cried Eddie, the youngest, a boy of eight years old, the pet and darling of all the five sisters.

"Tomorrow evening!" said Fannie, the next in order, "tomorrow evening. Oh, such fun. A Christmas tree!"

"Won't it be fun to dress it!" whispered Grace.

"Oh, Marian, will it have my work box?" cried Hester.

"And my doll?" said Fannie.

"And my set of china tea things? You know you promised me a new set." And fairly started, all the children joined in the list of demands, making a perfect Babel of the parlor.

The little mantel clock struck nine. As the last stroke died away, Marian pointed with a smile to the clock, and the children rose, kissed their sisters, and went merrily upstairs to bed, Fannie leading Eddie, while Hester and Lizzie, little girls of eleven and twelve, went up arm in arm.

"There is so much to do tomorrow, Gracie," said Marian, as the chamber door closed, shutting out the sound of the merry voices, "there are so many things to attend to that I think we will dress the tree this evening. We can shut the folding doors and keep the children from the back parlor tomorrow."

"Oh, yes, we will dress it now. I'll call father." And the young girl danced off, humming a merry tune. Marian, in the meantime, went out to a closet in the entry and brought in a large baize covering for the center of the floor. It was green, and meant for the foundation of the beautiful show Marian's tree always made. Grace and the Doctor soon came in, and the process of making a Christmas tree commenced in good earnest.

The square of green baize being tacked down, a large stone jar was placed in the middle of it, and in this the tree stood nobly erect. Damp sand was put round the stem till the large green tree stood firmly in its place. A flounce of green chintz round the jar concealed its stony ugliness, and over the top,

round the tree, was a soft cushion of moss. It was a large evergreen, reaching almost to the high ceiling, for all the family presents were to be placed upon it.

This finished, the process of dressing commenced. From a basket in the corner, Marian drew long strings of bright red holly berries threaded like beads upon fine cord. These were festooned in graceful garlands from the boughs of the tree, and while Marian was thus employed, Grace and the Doctor arranged the tiny tapers. This was a delicate task. Long pieces of fine wire were passed through the taper at the bottom, and these clasped over the stem of each branch and twisted together underneath. Great care was taken that there should be a clear space above each wick, that nothing might catch fire. Strings of bright berries, small bouquets of paper flowers, strings of beads, tiny flags of gay ribbons, stars and shields of gilt paper, lace bags filled with colored candies, knots of bright ribbons, all homemade by Marian's and Grace's skilful fingers, made a brilliant show at a very trifling cost, the basket seeming possessed of unheard of capacities, to judge from the multitude and variety of articles the sisters drew from it. Meantime, upon the wick of each little taper the Doctor rubbed with his finger a drop of alcohol to insure its lighting quickly. This was a process he trusted to no one else, for fear the spirit might fall upon some part of the tree not meant to catch fire.

At last, all the contents of the basket were on the tree, and then the more important presents were brought down from an upper room. There were many large articles seemingly too clumsy for the tree, but Marian passed around them gay colored ribbons till they formed a basket work, and looped them over the branches till even Hester's work box looked graceful. Dolls for each of the little girls were seated on the boughs, and a large cart for Eddie, with two horses prancing before it, drove gayly among the top branches, as if each steed possessed the wings of Pegasus. On the moss beneath the branches Marian placed a set of wooden animals for Eddie, while from the topmost branch was suspended a gilded cage ready for the canary bird Dr. Grantley had purchased for the pet-loving

THE CHRISTMAS TREE.

Lizzie. Various mysterious packages, wrapped in paper and marked Grace, Marian, or Papa, were put aside, that all the delicious mystery of Christmas might be preserved. At length all was ready and, carefully locking the doors, the trio went up their respective rooms.

From *Godey's Lady's Book* for December 1860.

SANTA CLAUS'S BALL

ANONYMOUS

SANTA CLAUS had appointed this November night as a dress rehearsal for Christmas. It was an occasion when not the Dolls only, but very many others, denizens of Toyland, were expected. All, in fact, who could make it convenient to attend felt it to be a duty to do so. In fact, the invitation was almost peremptory. Santa Claus expected to hear from his spies, the Old Dolls, full accounts of the conduct and behavior of his little friends the Children, in order that he might know who deserved his rich prizes, and who might merit the traditional "rod in the stocking" as the penalty of their misbehavior. He also expected to hear from the same reliable sources what all the mothers, sisters, aunts, and cousins were doing with reference to assisting him; and for this information he was accustomed to rely entirely upon the Dolls. They are a very intelligent race of little beings, if one did but know it, and they always sleep with at least one eye open. Con-

sequently, when the Children have gone to bed, and the Dolls set in order in the nursery, and the hidden work is taken out, and the mysterious plans of the family talked over, the Dolls have the best possible chance to see and hear it all, and of course their sympathies are all interested in the Children, and all that concerns them.

Santa Claus was accustomed to hold this annual festival preparatory to Christmas, in order to know exactly what to do, and what to depend upon.

The gala was held in Santa Claus's favorite winter palace, an immense snow cave in the side of Mount Hecla. Santa Claus found the climate to agree better with his health than a more southern situation, and likewise he found here the quiet and seclusion so necessary to the mystery in which he is accustomed to invest his good deeds.

The palace was all of a glow with warmth and light from numerous fires in huge fireplaces, whose vent was none less than the great crater of Hecla himself. The cheerful blaze illumined the glittering ceiling and spar-

kling walls, and mellowed the atmosphere to almost tropical geniality; while, to restrain the melting of snow and ice, which naturally would have ensued, and which would have greatly incommoded the guests, the palace was placed under a perpetual spell or charm by a certain witch. This witch when young had been a famous beauty, and a great favorite of the good saint, who was a gay bachelor in those days.

Of course she could not preside publicly at his entertainments; but it was more than surmised in Northern circles that his domestic *ménage* owed much to her occasional care. It was positively asserted that if she chose she could tell what had become of a certain Geyser, which had mysteriously disappeared of late, and there were not wanting dark hints that it had been placed in his kitchen by her agency, in order that he might enjoy a perpetual supply of hot water for his punch of which it was feared he was becoming very fond.

It is certain that he has been known to lay his finger aside his jolly red nose, wink oracularly, and indulge in a silent inward laugh and chuckle when the subject has been broached to him. But it is not my business to pry into the domestic concerns of these excellent people, but to give an account of Santa Claus's ball.

The dancing hall was brilliantly illuminated by certain Northern Lights, which had generously volunteered their services for the occasion, and a great number of Shooting Stars were engaged to act as drivers and torch bearers to convoy the guests to and from the scene of the festivities. It was expected that this evening would witness the *debut* of many of the belles and beaux of Toyland, and no pains or expense was spared to make the ball the affair of the season.

Santa Claus had dispatched his numerous reindeer teams over the American continent to collect his guests; and, lest these accommodations should fail, several Lapland witches had benevolently loaned their broomsticks for the use of such of the company who might prefer them. Jack Frost had done himself more than justice in the upholstery and finishing of the palace, which he could well afford to do, having had the contract from time immemorial. The tables were abundantly spread with viands suited to the tastes and appetites of the guests; while Boreas was engaged to furnish music, assisted by a large deputation of Tin Trumpets and Painted Drums, who were expected to arrive somewhat later in the evening.

Santa Claus had to hear what communications his emissaries might have for him, and this must be attended to before dancing, of course.

The apartments were decorated with hemlock boughs and garlands, brought thither with infinite pains. Ashberries and holly, with the ancient mistletoe, were tastefully arranged over the walls, and huge sparkling icicles glittered among them in pure and beautiful contrast to the rich dark-green of the evergreens.

The reception room was thickly carpeted with Iceland moss for the benefit of rheumatic old Dolls, and to enable imprudent young lady Dolls who might have overheated themselves with dancing to resort thither and save themselves a pulmonary attack by inhaling its health-restoring fragance.

And now, as everything had been properly attended to, and the arrangements were to his entire satisfaction, the old gentleman, in his best suit of furs, with his pipe laid aside for once, in compliment to the ladies, stood before the great fireplace in the reception room, with his back to the fire and his coat tails judiciously drawn on each side, awaiting the arrival of his visitors. He did not have to wait long; for the tinkle of his reindeers' bells were now heard, and the first installment of Dolls soon entered the apartment.

As he expected, they were the invalid guard of the ball, the battered and disabled ones, who had stood one year, at least, of the Nursery campaign, and their battered noses, cracked crowns, and shattered or missing limbs bore evidence to the hard service they had seen.

Polly, the oldest Doll, opened the conversation with grumbling and complaints. She was a very old Doll. Lame and dilapidated, with one arm and a foot gone, and her frock torn half off her shoulders, and her garments soiled and tattered generally, she presented but a sorry appearance.

After extending a courteous welcome to the lame, halt, and blinded party, he lent a listening ear to her grievances.

"If your highness could only know of the goings on in our nursery. Now I don't come here to complain of neglect or ill-usage like some, though I was once a very handsome china Doll, and was dressed and petted as much as the best. Nor do I complain of my broken arm"; and she sadly held up the stump of her once plump and snow-white arm. "But it is not myself," she went on, wiping her remaining eye with a soiled rag of a handkerchief; "it's the Children I'm so sorry for. Why, their mother *never* comes into the nursery more than once a day, and often not that. Sometimes she sweeps in in splendid carriage-dress just ready for a drive, and just touches the children, with 'There, there! don't touch my dress'; and off she goes, while the Children stand at the window and cry themselves sick to see the carriage go off, in which they very seldom have a ride, and never with mamma, unless she goes to fit them with clothes and hats.

"And when little Mary had the scarlet fever, she left some tiny pills with Kate, the Irish nurse, and told her to give them so often, and the child would be well enough in the morning. But Mary worried and fretted for mamma, who was away at a grand party, and Katy was sleepy and tired, and she muttered to herself—*I* heard her—'What's the use o' bothering wi' the like of this thrash! I'll just be giving the poor thing a dhrop o' suthin' to bring the slape to her eyes.' And she *did* give her something out of a bottle, and Mary never woke up out of that sleep. And they carried her away, and I never saw her again. Mary had me in her little bed all the time, and I know all about it."

"How many children are there left?" asked Santa Claus, blowing his nose very hard.

"Two," answered Polly; "another girl and a teething baby. I know just how many teeth he has, for he tries 'em all on me, and I know the minute one is through."

"Poor little things!" sighed the good saint; "I really do not see how I can help them. Is there no aunt or cousin in the house?"

"Yes. Aunt Sophia and Cousin Bell; but they are entirely taken up with Aid Societies, and Lint Circles, and Hospital visiting, and they have no time for the poor children. Mrs. Harvey, the mamma, is wiser. She gave ten dollars to escape the trouble."

"Not so bad! not so bad!" exclaimed the host. "I rejoice that my friends the soldiers are to fare so well. May the shirts be warm and the turkeys fat that I bring, that is all! I don't suppose there is much chance that my juvenile friends are being calculated upon at all, is there?"

"Not much. I fancy the Soldiers' Christmas box engrosses all their time and attention, and the children always come off second to the public in that house."

"The poor children! the poor children!" put in another doll. "Now where I live there are four little children, and not a rag of new clothes have those poor young ones had this fall or winter, and no prospect of them. And not for lack of money either. Mamma is away to the Hospital, or the Aid Society, or the Lint Company, or what not, as soon as she gets her breakfast, and Tommy's face isn't washed, nor Lizzie's hair curled until the middle of the afternoon, when Betty is all done her work. The cook hasn't made a seed cake this fall, and every thing nice of jellies or fruit, or whatever there is, goes to the soldiers. The children don't know what a kiss or a story is hardly, it's so long since they heard one; and Charlie's shoes have gaped for patches this month, and Molly's hat is a sight to behold."

"Well, but," interposed the saint, "the soldiers are proper subjects for care and kindness. They need jellies and the children don't; and, poor fellows! they have no mothers to wait upon them."

"Small loss if they are like some mothers I know; but if these mothers don't train and love their own little soldiers at home, there will be another great rebellion one of these days."

"Just my notion," mumbled an old nutcracker. "If the Southron mothers had only cared for their children when they were little instead of always *threatening* to send them to convents or boarding-schools—and finally *doing* it to get rid of the trouble they ought *them-selves* to take—South Carolina never would have seceded, and Master Peyton wouldn't have screwed my neck off with rage when he heard of the victory of Fort Donelson."

There was another loud jingle of bells, and a merry load of the aristocrats of Toyland were joyfully ushered in. They were accompanied by a Zouave, whose pretty china head and brilliant red white and blue had evidently dazzled the eyes of all the female portion of the company—all but Miss Josephine. She, the waxen beauty in her silk and blond, her tarletan and spangles, her embroidery and lace, felt herself entitled to the belleship of the ballroom without a question, and was especially irritated at the company of certain nondescript Dolls, who were exceedingly presumptuous, as she deemed it, in riding in the same sleigh as herself. She was especially conceited on the subject of her birth; for, as she boasted, she was a genuine Parisian, body, complexion, curls, dress, and all; and, moreover, a true Santa Clausian, who had come down standing in Santa Claus's own hands, and was none of your fair-bought, homemade, homedressed, got-up-any-how affairs. She had been promenaded on the Boulevards, and aired in the Bois de Boulogne, and was bursting with spite that the Zouave, who was, as she alleged, "only bought at a Soldiers' Fair," should not notice her more than he did.

She flirted her tarletans contemptuously past him, and courtesied to the ground before the host. He greeted her kindly, and courteously inquired the occasion of her clouded brow.

"I can not bear mixed companies," she answered with ill-concealed disdain.

"But my invitation was peremptory."

"True, and therefore am I here."

"Yet, my pretty Doll, your countenance indicates that you come reluctantly."

The petted beauty burst into tears.

"May I never become human!" she exclaimed. "If my heart is not almost broken with neglect!"

(This is the hoped-for future of Dolls, and with good reason, for the metamorphosis is well authenticated in many cases.)

"Neglect! I supposed the fair Josephine was far above the danger of neglect!" murmured the Zouave.

"It is very well for you, Colonel Ellsworth, to speak in that way," she pettishly replied. "You know that I have lain in the drawer without a breath of air or glimpse of daylight but what comes through the broken lock of my drawer, while you sit in the Doll chair, the pet and darling of the nursery, and feel yourself Lord Paramount every where. My *worst* trouble, and the cause of all my troubles, is the ambition of my little mistress's parents. Unfortunately she let it out that she was a bright child, and they have shown her no mercy ever since. She goes to school at half past eight every morning. She remains until half past two, then she comes home, eats a lunch, and practices music until four. Then she sews an hour for the Aid Societies, then her evening meal and lessons from seven till nine, when my poor ten-year-old mistress goes to bed. Every day of the week this is the rule except Saturday, when sewing for the soldiers takes the place of lessons at school, and maybe she gets a short walk in the afternoon.

"Dear Santa Claus, can not you help us? She will die if this goes on. I see and hear this, and it is every word of it true"; and the tears stood again—tender, loving tears—in her waxen blue eyes.

The saint's eyes glowed like sparks under his shaggy eyebrows.

"My Master greatly loved these little ones when he dwelt on the earth, and if their human parents do not more carefully watch and tend them he will gather the lambs to his bosom again," he murmured softly to himself, as he slowly paced the floor, with his hands contemplatively clasped under his coattails.

A brisk-looking jointed Chinese Doll now hopped up to their host, and began to retail both information and grievance in his attentive ear.

She said that she and her friends Hoop and Hoopstick, Ball and Bat, Battle-door and Shuttle-cock, were under a ban, and were heartbroken at the aspect of things in their residence, which was in Boston. She really did not see how she was going to bear it any longer. Evening study was now the rule, and the poor children went to bed so tired that when they rose in the morning they had no spirits for play at all, neither had they the time. She

couldn't remember when they had had time.

Katy was as pale as a ghost trying for the prize for French, and Milly was equally desperate for the mathematical medal. She stated that her memory couldn't recall when she had been properly undressed and put to bed, and she had quite lost her voice, it was so long since she had been squeezed.

The circle smiled at this, and the Zouave mischievously encircled her waist with his padded arm, to which pressure she responded with an extremely natural "squawk," which proved her bellows in excellent order, and made the Dolls look scandalized behind their fans, and Miss Josephine walked away as haughty as a crowned queen.

"It seems that the Aid Societies do not trouble your house very much," whispered the Zouave, offering his arm for a promenade; "at least you do not oppose them as violently as many do."

"Ah!" sighed the almond-eyed Squaw Lin, accepting the proffered arm with a mollified air, "if all soldiers were like Colonel Ellsworth! But really, if you *could* only see the wooden German Grenadiers at our house which came home from the last fancy fair—" The rest of the sentence was lost as they sauntered off to try the flavor of an ice *à la Hecla.*

Santa Claus looked after them with a peculiar smile.

"We have all been young once," he sighed. "I had a touch of the complaint many years ago myself."

There were many complaints and much important information brought to Santa Claus that night, to all of which he attentively listened, and promised to use his influence on the side of right, reserving to himself the privilege of judging the merits of the case.

There were almost universal complaint from the city Dolls that their little mistresses were overstudied, in school and out of school; and although the complaint came selfishly from the Dolls, Santa Claus knew too well the consequences to pass the information in silence. Dull children were in little danger. It was the bright, talented ones, who needed no urging to study at all, to whom the harm happened. Boys could and would get air and exercise somehow; but little girls, bright, studious, lady-

SANTA CLAUS'S BALL

like little girls, had no redress if parents did
not take up their cause.

Santa Claus had a theory that, if a little girl
of ten years old made the clothes for her Doll
family, it was about as much sewing as she
ought to be expected to do; and if she was studious in school she ought not to be expected
to study out of school and give up her play
hours. He espoused the cause of the Hoops and
Balls, the Battle-doors and Shuttle-cocks, feeling that they had a good work to do, in which
the parents ought rather to aid than restrain
them.

His "little ones" were especially dear to the
saint's heart, and he believed that his little Peter
Parlegians had turned out full as well as those
whose studies were more pretentious. He sadly
remembered certain bright little faces that, one
Christmas, would peer so curiously and sweetly
into the stockings it had been his care to fill for
them, who, before another Christmas, had laid
their throbbing heads and quivering nerves to
rest where schoolbooks should never annoy
them more. And he shrewdly opined that if

half the amount of study at present exacted
was performed in school under the teacher's
eye, and with his assistance, the good results
mentally would be doubled; and if the time
thus saved from study be devoted to vigorous
romping in doors or out, the value to the little students would be wonderful, and the bright
eyes and curls might look into well-filled stockings until years insensibly stole away the child's
privilege. But Santa Claus sighed deeply when
he thought how hopeless was the task of con-
vincing parents of this.

His heart grew still heavier when he thought
of the many nurseries unblessed by the constant presence of a mother. Society—gay, be-
witching, fascinating society—claimed so many,
especially young mothers. "And yet," he reflected, as he promenaded the now nearly deserted reception-room, and the gusty sounds
of distant music reached his ears from the
dancing halls, where the Tin Trumpet Band,
Boreas conductor, discoursed melody for the
multitude of twinkling feet—"and yet this class
are not so hopeless after all; for sooner or

later sorrow, steadiness, or wisdom come to all, and these gay young creatures turn out pretty well after all; for most generally it is only an excess of animal spirits which passes off in time. It's only a few comparatively—alas that there should be any!—who are incorrigible." But even Santa Claus shook his head as he reflected that so many really excellent, high-principled, kind-hearted mothers find their duties and tastes leading them away from home and the dear faces there, even to the neglect of his darling pets, who so sadly missed the smile, the kiss, the story or romp, the walk or ride with mamma, the sunshine of her presence. And very sad remembrances occurred to him of those who, having no tender drawing out of love of home, found bright fires and lights (such unhallowed ones!) elsewhere, and sweet smiles and brilliant glances, glowing with no holy mother-love, and accepted the wretched substitutes. He loved the poor soldiers; they were his especial care. Many a box of comforts and delicacies had he conveyed to them, and so joyfully, when mothers, sisters, and daughters filled them; but his heart ached for the dear Children whose mothers, in restlessness or ignorance, had neglected them to minister to strangers. He saw in this very neglect, whether from misguided ambition or simply indolence, the one great cause of the Great Rebellion; for, of a certainty, if the Children can obey well, the men will command well, and deserve well of the opinion of the world.

The Children of Santa Claus must neither be left to the exclusive care of either Biddy or Dinah. Neither devoted to death upon the school desk, nor impaled by the needles of infanticidal Sewing Societies. The races and romps, the balls and hoops, must resume their rule. Their precious Doll cares and baby housekeeping, the song or story from mamma, the evening frolic with papa, must be reinstated. Bo-Peep and Cock Robin must not be supplanted by Manesea and Davies, nor Jack the Giant Killer by Dumas or De Staël, nor Mother Goose by Watts on the Mind. Not a bit of it. And St. Nicholas swore by his eight favorite reindeer to claim back his own, and bid the children be Children once more.

He resolved that the children of soldiers, either absent or killed, should fare especially well, and their stockings well filled by hook or crook, and re-resolved that within the circle of his influence all faces should be bright and happy—Aid Society or Gay Society to the contrary, notwithstanding.

So he walked along with his hands in his pockets to watch the dancers. They were holding high revel there. Over the glittering floor they flew, waxen beauties, clasped by stalwart Highlander or courtly Louis Quatorze, who had escaped from the drawing-room mantles. Bronze knights in armor clinked their mailed heels in time with plump china Dolls. Rag Dolls waddled round in the embrace of India-rubber Zouaves. Wooden Dolls stumped round in the Mazurka with the German Grenadiers. Hideous Gutta Perchas and half naked Arabs hob-a-nobbed with Walnut witches over their boiling punch; while Jumping Jacks executed frantic polkas with beautiful dancing Dolls; and Chinese Dolls and Crying Babies squalled vigorously, as energetic Harlequins bounced them around in time to the wild music of the Band. The Northern Lights glimmered and flashed, the huge fire-places glowed with fervent heat. The icicles trembled on the garlands, and the weird music played faster and faster, and round and round they flew under its enchantment. The Sister of Charity, her skirts smeared with the ink she had wiped from numerous pens, simpered slyly under her big white bonnet, as she touched glasses with a burly Punch, astride a beer cask. She looked abominably knowing as she winked to him that she could, if she chose, reveal what a soldier in camp had written under her supervision. "That is, I sat on the inkstand, and wiped his pen—so I read his letter," and she smiled as a gay young tiger replenished her glass with the hottest of punch.

I should talk forever to describe every thing said and done that night. I shall only hint how certain Dolls, too old to dance and too young to stay at home, formed in a snug whist party, and *en masse* got gloriously fuddled, insomuch that some ventured too close to the fire and were instantly reduced to glowing charcoal; while others, not discerning the difference between a witch's broomstick and a comfortable sleigh, imprudently chose the former, and while in the act of sailing home, singing

"On the bat's back do I fly!"

incontinently tumbled off and were lost in the Arctic ocean, and never heard from more. The younger portion of the company, who drank only ice water, all got home in perfect safety before cock crow.

Santa Claus made a speech to the Dolls, in which "he assured the Dolls that he would attend to their grievances, and see to it that they had more of the time and attention of their little mistresses than ever before; also that a flea should be judiciously inserted into the ears of the mothers, to the intent that their assistance and co-operation should be lent to further his plans for a merry Christmas. He added that the soldiers were the fathers of his children, and had been his children themselves, and should receive his especial care and attention. All that could be done for them was right, except when it robbed little ones of their mothers. Likewise, the children and orphans of soldiers were under his especial care, and he promised to co-operate with all Dolls from Fancy Fairs, to see that they were placed where they would do most good to the children."

He squeezed Polly's remaining hand, and exhorted her to mind the slippery steps, and pinched Josephine's glowing cheek, as she curtsied before him down to the ground and showered her flaxen curls over her waxen beauty; she leaned on the arm of the Ellsworth Zouave, who tenderly wrapped her white opera cloak around her, as he placed her inside the sleigh and took his own seat on the box beside the strolling Star who acted as driver for the nonce.

He comforted Squaw Lin, who looked venomously after them as they departed, with a promise of a splendid guttapercha Uncle Tom, and laughed himself sore to see her look of disgust.

He felt an inward disquiet, though he could not keep his face straight either, as he saw that the Walnuts and Gutta Perchas had had more than was good for them, and more than doubtful if all of them would arrive safe home.

He detained the demure Sister of Charity a moment with a whispered hint of caution un-

der her bonnet, and gave her arm a sly pinch as she nodded so violently that she nearly lost her headgear. There was a secret understanding between them, only to be divulged to you, dear reader.

He watched each guest depart, and the long train of matrons, each escorting a load of merry, sleepy, tired Dolls home to their nursery, streamed across the ebon sky like a procession of sparks from a great conflagration.

They were the happiest Dolls that ever started off to a midnight frolic, and the tipsy ones made their exit singing,

"Wewongohomt'llmo'n'g,
'T'lldayltdoespear!"

Then he went in, lighted his pipe, and sat down to cogitate before his fire till morning. Then he concluded that an account of his ball had better be sent to *Harper's Weekly,* and see if a plea for the Children could not be made through its pages; and I did it for him, and here is the story.

Harper's Weekly, January 3, 1863.

THE TOY-SELLER'S CHRISTMAS

You would hardly fancy that selling Christmas gifts was an occupation to breed melancholy, and yet Simeon Golding had found it so. Ever since the rush began to buy presents he had grown more and more sad; until, when the 24th of December came, and all the world was out buying things for the morrow, he felt a desperate impulse to leave his shop to take care of itself, and go away somewhere, any where, to get out of the sight and sound of all this gladness in which he had no share. You would never have taken Simeon Golding for a man of sentiment—nobody thought that of him of all the people who had bought holiday presents for ten years in his gay little shop on Broadway. If people thought of him at all, it was as an honest, dull fellow, an obliging shopman, who minded his own business, and was pretty sure to have on hand just what any one wanted—sure, also, not to forget orders or disappoint customers. If you had told them that he was an old bachelor, very likely they would have smiled, and said, "I thought as much. His whole mind is in his business, you see. That's what makes him so careful and punctual.—It's the best toy-shop in the city."

But for a man whose whole mind was in his business this mood of Simeon's was a strange one. He scarcely knew himself how it had grown on him so overmasterly. He had always felt something of it at holiday time— just a sense of lonesomeness. It made him remember, you know, how solitary *he* was when he saw so many surprises prepared—so many tokens of thought and care for wives, and children, and husbands, and lovers—and remembered that for him no Christmas gifts would wait. No gentle woman's voice would wish him "Merry Christmas!" No clamorous children would throng round him with their noisy pleasure. But hitherto it had all ended as it had begun in this vague lonesomeness; the mood had never overpowered him as it had done this year, making him for the first time almost unequal to the demands upon him, and humiliating him in the eyes of his assistants, whom he had held in awe hitherto by his superior capacity and readiness. Is it, I wonder, that we feel the presence of Fate long before she stands beside us—that vague hints of coming events are in the air, and the strange restlessness for which we can not account is the stirring of the soul at some presence felt ere yet it is seen?

Simeon Golding was past forty. Far back in the morning land of youth lay all his old dreams, and hopes, and loves. It was strange how near they had seemed to him this year since the preparations for Christmas commenced. He needed only to close his eyes on city sights, his ears on city sounds, to feel himself a boy once more. He lived all those early years over again—years in which he was the one joy and hope in life to his widowed mother. *Then* some one cared for him. *Then* no Christmas went by without its gifts. He remembered how the very thing he wanted was sure to come; and how he used to earn money by stealth to be able to give *her* some token of merry Christmas. He saw her, looking back, so plainly—that gentle woman to whom sorrow, patiently borne, had taught lessons of sainthood—saw her sitting by the fire with pale, placid face, and hair where grief, not years, had sown threads of silver; but yet, in spite of all, with a smile always bright for him, and a heart young enough and cheery enough always to joy in his joy. Oh! what would he give now for one of those well-remembered smiles, one touch of that gentle hand! He had been nearly twenty-five years old when she died; but just as much his mother's boy as the day his father had left him to her keeping. He wondered to feel the tears filling his eyes—eyes that wept so seldom—as the memory of that great loss swept over him: the still, still face; the dear, stirless lips that would never smile more; the hands folded dumbly on the breast, like a saint's in some trance of prayer; and then the open grave, the lowered coffin, and the earth dropping on it solemnly, with the pale November sunshine overhead, and the dead leaves soaked with moisture at his feet.

It was in the dark days which followed that the sun of his life arose, and he loved with the one pure and perfect passion of which his being was capable—the ripe fruit of his

THE TOY SHOP.

whole manhood. He remembered how he had seen *her* first—that girl so bright and so bonny! He recalled her dark eyes, which seemed kindled sometimes by an interior light, like the flame which glows through the heart of an opal; which at other times were full of a brooding melancholy that stirred his heart even more than their brightness. He remembered the clear, dark complexion, with its rich, glowing coloring; the heavy-falling black hair; the bright, wayward face, with its full, pouting lips, and its expression self-willed, yet wonderfully beguiling. How well he had loved her, without one thought whether she could return it

99

or not. Looking back, he did not wonder at this love; nor was he sorry for it—all in vain as it had proved. She had rejected his suit, not unkindly, but with an air and manner which made him feel how utterly impossible it was that she could care for him. And then he had gone away from the little country village, and had never gone back since, not even to look at his mother's grave. What need, when she was buried in his heart, and all her truth and tenderness commemorated there as on a monument?

He had never heard about *her* any more— that bright enchantress of his young manhood! He had never cared to hear. If she loved and married some one else afterward he did not want to know it; and perhaps this was why he had kept away from Hillsboro. Five years he had served in another man's toy-shop, and then he had opened this one of his own: where, as the phrase goes, he had done well. And now he was past forty, and all alone, and Christmas was coming on.

He had never cared for any woman since that dark, bright vision had dawned, star-like, in his sky, and set again for him forever. Nor was this from any high-flown notions of constancy or sentiment. He had not resolved never to love again—or, indeed, speculated about it at all. Simply, he was just one of those men whose nature never blossoms but once. So he looked forward to nothing—nothing, that is, beyond his present life. He had looked at himself in the glass that morning, and noted how strong and tough of fibre he was—noted the plain, rugged outlines of face and figure—and thought resignedly that he was good for at least twenty years more of hard work. He would make all the money he could, and then, when he died, give it to someone who needed it, whom it would make happier, and who would therefore think of his memory sometimes with tender gratitude. Who this someone should be he did not know, but he would find out by-and-by. You see he was not a man of expanded benevolence, this toy seller. He never made any large schemes. His money would not go to missions, or tract societies, or hospitals. He dealt in small things always, and he just wanted to raise himself a monument in some one grateful heart. And the day went

on, the strange restlessness he could not shake off overpowered him, and the burden of his solitary life pressed upon him more heavily, and it was afternoon.

He was standing behind the counter, idle for a moment, though there was no lack of customers in the shop on whom the rest were waiting. He had forgotten where he was until a voice recalled him.

"If you please, Sir, is there any thing pretty which I could buy for a quarter of a dollar?"

There was something in the voice which sounded to him like an echo of his dreams. He looked at the speaker in a bewildered way, as if he were not quite sure whether he were awake. Was he twenty-five years old again and in Hillsboro? Here were the dark, slumberous eyes, the heavy-falling hair, the rich tints of cheek and lip that had lived all these years in his memory. But the figure was smaller. This girl at his counter was twelve, perhaps, and the simplicity of childhood was in her look. Still he had almost called her, before he thought, by the name of that early vision, the spell of the past was so strong upon him. She repeated her timid question, and he bent toward her then, fully in possession of his faculties, alert to the demands of the occasion.

"Is it for yourself?" he asked.

"No, for my mother. She is very ill, and we have so little money that I can spend but this, which is my own. I want so to make her a Christmas present. Is there any thing that I can buy?"

He laid before her some trifles, each one worth several times her quarter, but small and simple enough to convey to an undiscriminating child the idea of cheapness.

"Any of these you can buy," he said, kindly.

She selected a tiny Parian vase, just large enough for a single rose-bud, and gave him her piece of currency. He wrapped up the vase lingeringly in a soft paper. How could he lose sight of her, he thought, so like as she was to *her?* Then, too, perhaps he could help her. He gathered courage from the exigency of the situation.

"Did you say your mother was ill?" he asked.

"Very ill, Sir!"

"You have other friends, of course?" And then, seeing the surprised look on her face, he explained, "Don't think I'm curious or impertinent, only you are so like a very dear friend I had once that I can not bear to part with you if there is any chance, the least chance, that I could do any thing—for that old friend's sake, you know—to make your Christmas any happier."

When he had said this he paused, frightened at the impulsiveness which he found in himself still, this man of forty. The girl had an unusual amount of penetration for her years. She flashed a searching glance at him, and made up her mind that he was an honest and a good man, who meant just what he said —no less, no more.

"We have no friends," she said, slowly, "except the doctor, who comes to see my mother, and is very kind. My father came to New York a year ago, to get into business, and died soon after. We have lived since partly on the money he left us, and partly on what my mother earned by embroidery. But now, for several weeks, she has been too ill to work."

"Then may I come to see her? There might be some way in which I could help you, and I *wish* I could, for the sake of that dear friend who was so like you."

"Thank you, Sir. I know my mother will be glad to see you. You will find us at No. 11 Carmine Street. My mother is Mrs. Reynolds."

"I will come this evening," he said, as he handed her the little vase. "I will not be later than I can help; but to-day, you know, we are very busy."

She smiled with a bright smile, Marian Varick's own smile, and went out. He stood a moment wondering at himself. What connection was there likely to be between this unknown Mrs. Reynolds and the Marian Varick to whom he had bidden good-by fifteen years ago, in that little New Hampshire town? And yet those eyes and that hair—were there many such faces in this world? He did not feel so solitary any more. He had an interest now; he too. He began to serve customers briskly, with his old, cheery manner.

But at seven o'clock he left the shop. Never had he done such a thing before since he first commenced business as to leave his shop to his subordinates on the night before Christmas. But, careful man as he was, he felt urged on

by some power apart from himself so that he could not wait for the lagging hours. He arranged matters as well as he could, thankful that people whom he could trust were about him—went home for a hurried supper, a hurried adjustment of linen and neck-tie, and then took his way across the city. Twice he stopped, once at a bookseller's, where he bought an elegant volume—for he was too delicate, this sandy-haired, dull-looking man, whom no one suspected of delicacy, to make gifts out of his own shop—and once at a florist's, where he purchased the most exquisite rose-bud he could find. He stood in Carmine Street at last, rang the bell at the door of No. 11, and inquired for Mrs. Reynolds.

"Two flights up—the back room," the woman answered, civilly; and he went up the stairs.

Before the door of the room he paused a moment, with that strange, overmastering feeling which comes to one sometimes in the great crises of life. He could scarcely breathe. He did not know *what* he expected, but he felt Fate was at his side leading him on. He knocked at the door at last, and the girl whom he had seen at his shop opened it. Standing there on the threshold he saw one sight only— a woman's face on the pillows—a face with crimson flushes on the olive cheeks, with great, dark, sad eyes and heavy-falling hair—Marian Varick's own. Her glance met his, and the color in her cheeks deepened. She spoke first.

"Are you the friend, Simeon Golding, whom God has raised up for me at my sore need? Have you forgiven me the pain I caused you once?"

"There was no need to forgive you, Marian," the man said, humbly—"no need. I was glad to have known what love was, even though it was all in vain. I have never loved any one since, and I thank God that He has brought me to you at last."

"It is indeed at last," she said, "for I am counting my life now by hours. The doctor said so this afternoon, while she, poor child, was gone out"; and her fond eyes rested on the girl at her bed's foot. "She knows it now, and she is trying to be calm and strong for my sake."

The toy-seller glanced at the stand beside the bed, and saw the little white vase on it. She had not dared keep it till the morrow, poor child, lest morrow for her mother there should be none. He took his rose-bud from its soft cotton wrappings and put it into the vase silently. The book he would not offer—it was no time for Christmas tokens other than flowers, such as one might fancy would bloom in another world as well as in this. Mrs. Reynolds looked at the rose with eyes that had loved and rejoiced in beauty all her life long.

"It was so good of you to fetch it," she said. "It makes me think of Hillsboro. You used always to bring me roses there, you know."

Yes, he knew, but to him, seeing her so changed, it seemed ages since then. She understood his faraway look.

"Yes, it was long since," she answered to his thought. "I have loved since then, and I have lost, and now I am going home."

He wondered to see her so calm—to see the child so calm also—to be so calm himself, when the only woman he had ever loved lay dying. It was God's peace, he thought, resting on the scene, hushing their three hearts.

"Has your child any friends?" he asked, after a while.

"Only you."

"Then there is no one to whom I need give her up. Think, if you could have loved me she might have been mine. Will you give her to me now? It will make amends for all losses. I am able to care for her. I will be faithful to your trust."

"Yes, yours was always a faithful soul," she murmured. "Marian, child, will you go with Mr. Golding when I am gone?"

For a moment a great sob strangled the girl's utterance, but she conquered it bravely, and answered to the entreaty in her mother's eyes:

"Yes, mother."

"Go with him, dear, and be as good a child to him as you have been to me. Let him never be lonely in the world any more."

"Yes, mother."

Then they were all silent, and the moments went on so fast, so fast!

The hours passed from nine o'clock till mid-night. Now and then the mother spoke some word of fond, lingering love to her child, or of gratitude to her other watcher; but, for the most part, all was still. At last they heard the clock in a neighboring belfry strike, and the dying woman counted the twelve strokes. A smile flitted like the ghost of her old brightness across her face.

"See!" she said, "it is Christmas, and I give you my Christmas gift. From today Marian shall be your daughter."

He took in his the girl's hand, which those cold fingers placed there, taking upon him so a solemn vow. From henceforth the welfare of Marian Reynolds would be his life's end and aim. She would be to him in place of the own children he was never to see at his fireside. Having her, he would not miss them. Having her, he would never be lonely or solitary any more. For him, as for other men, Christmas would have a meaning. There would be one for him to make happy—one for whom to toil, and save, and live, ay, die if need were—for it meant all this to that faithful, honest soul when he took his adopted child, his Christmas gift, from Marian Varick's dying hand.

At last the night wore toward the morning. The keen, penetrating cold which just precedes the dawn chilled them. A faint pink began to flush the sky. The mother looked up, with the crimson dying on her cheeks, the light fading from her eyes, and whispered to her child:

"Today I shall keep my Christmas with your father in the land of the angels. Good-by, my darling!" Then she looked into Simeon Golding's eyes, and said with tones so low that he had to bend very near to catch them—"My friend, you have been faithful unto death."

And then the dawn light came in—"the morn of the Nativity had just begun to break."

Mr. Golding rose and put out the night lamp. When he came back to the bedside he saw the eyes from which the soul no longer looked, the hands falling dumbly, and knew that Marian Varick, in the hush of the Christmas dawning, had gone home, and for her the Heavenly morning "had just begun to break."

From *Harper's Weekly.*

OUT IN THE COLD

HOLLY BERRIES

A Confederate Christmas Story
BY REFUGITTA

AH, WHAT A BITTER NIGHT! Great guns of wind went booming down the street, hustling round the corners, and spending their fury upon the naked shivering tree tops. All through the day had that strife gone on until dusk began, and then the strife ceased, and the heavens prepared to hang out their flag of truce in the shape of a heavy snow all ready against the morrow—for it was Christmas Eve, and what would a Christmas Day be without snow-balls?

I wonder if all the happy little darlings who, well wrapped and shielded from the frost nips, trooped through the streets that day, had any idea that there were some children as young and as fond of fun as themselves not many squares away who never had heard of a plum pudding, and knew if they were to hang up their poor little stockings every night of the year there was not a Santa Claus to put so much as a mint stick into them!

Well, it does seem hard to cloud over those sunshiny faces with such a doleful picture of holiday times—so just to cheer ourselves up, let us turn round this corner and join that crowd of don't care little ragamuffins staring in at Mr. Pin's grocery shop window. I know it will make your mouths water now, Confederate juveniles, to recall such a tempting array. There was, first, behind the clear crystal pane, a mammoth turkey, so fat that it must have submitted to be killed from sheer in-

103

ability to eat and move, hung all around with sausage balls and embowered in crisp white celery with its feathered tops. Many a belated housekeeper or father of a family, passing by, cast loving glances at the monster bird, and turned away with their hands on depleted purses and arms full of brown paper parcels. Then there were straw baskets of eggs, white and shining with the delightful prospect of translation into future eggnogs; pale yellow butter stamped with ears of corn, bee hives, and statuesque cows with their tails in an attitude. But these were all substantials, and the principal attraction was the opposite window, where great pyramids of golden oranges, scaly brown pineapples, festoons of bananas, boxes of figs and raisins with their covers thrown temptingly aside, foreign sauces and pickles, cheeses, and gilded walnuts were arranged in picturesque regularity, just, as it seemed, almost within reach of one's olfactories and mouth, until a closer proximity realized the fact of that thick plate glass between. Inside it was just the same: there were barrels and boxes in a perfect wilderness; curious old foreign packages and chests, savory of rare teas and rarer jellies; cinnamon odors like gales from Araby meeting you at every turn; but yet everything, from the shining mahogany counter under the brilliant gaslight, up to the broad, clean, round face of the jolly grocer Pin, was so neat and orderly and inviting that you felt inclined to believe yourself requested to come in and take off things by the pocketful, without paying a solitary cent.

I acknowledge that it was an unreasonable distribution of favors for Mr. Pin to own, all to himself, this abundance of good things. Now, in my opinion, little children ought to be the shop keepers when there are apples and oranges to be sold, and I know they will all agree with me, for I well remember my earliest ambition was that my papa would turn confectioner, and then I could eat my way right through the store. But our friend John Pin was an appreciative person, and not by any means forgetful of his benefits. All day long and throughout the short afternoon, his domain had been thronged with busy buyers, old and young, and himself and his assistant (a meager-looking young man of about the dimensions of a knitting needle) constantly employed in supplying their demands. John Pin's good nature never seemed to flag, and it would have done your heart good to see his tenderness with the little undecided children who, escorted by smiling nurses or mammas, and flourishing the silver half dollar they held ever so tight in their tiny fists, enquired the price of everything, from the japanned tea boxes down. One little boy, indeed, had quite a crying fit because he was not allowed to invest in and immediately devour a large jar of French mustard whose bright red label had happened to strike his fancy, and it was with much difficulty that Mr. Pin made peace through the medium of a nice fat fig. But the store was pretty nearly clear now, and as Mr. Pin put his head outside to note the progress of the weather, he ran into the group before mentioned, who scattered like a swarm of bees round one of his own hogsheads.

"Get out, you little rascals," said the good-natured John. "Here I came near breaking my neck over some of you, and that would have been a nice thing for this Christmas Eve, to be sure. I can't have you all blocking up the way of my customers," he added, turning back for a moment inside the door and coming out with a large basket, "so come here and hold out your double hands, all of you, and then run along home."

What a splendid hurrah went up over those nice nuts and raisins! Then John gave them each an apple from the barrel to his right, drove them all off cheerily, and went back, closing the door with a kindly bang.

He never noticed, nor did anyone else, the tiny little forlorn figure perched up on an empty sugar barrel under the window. It might have been one of the cherubs carved in stone, so motionless was the pose, but for the breath going out in rings upon the frosty air, and the heaving of the baby breast.

Perhaps John Pin's smile would not have been quite so broad as he went inside if he had seen the sad little picture; but as it was he rubbed his hands and, opening an inner door, cried out: "Mary, Mary!"

"Coming, father," answered a sweet child's voice, at the very sound of which John Pin's face was illuminated with love and pride; and directly after in came a little girl, delicate and brown-haired, dressed in some dark plaid stuff, with a little sprig of holly in the brooch fastening her narrow collar. A perfect home jewel she was; you did not need John Pin's eyes to tell you—so gentle and modest, yet so full of premature thought and care for the broad, bluff father, into whose arms she was at once lifted for a kiss.

"I called you, dear, to keep me company for a while. Reuben Thomas, your good mother, the widow, will be looking out for you, so I will take care of the store tonight. Don't stop to put up the shutters, but go right along. My respects and the good wishes of the season to Mrs. Thomas, both from me and my little Mary here. She is to come and eat Christmas fare with us tomorrow, don't forget. And here, sir—a few things for the children from Mary."

The poor young man's lean, dull face brightened as he took the hand extended and the basket at once. Well he knew that the "few things for the children" included many a delicacy unknown in the humble dwelling of his widowed mother—rarities that would cast completely in the shade his own present of tea paid for by the savings of many weeks gone by. Awkwardly enough his thanks, that so painfully embarrassed the grocer's honest self, were stammered out; and wrapping himself up in an overcoat certainly not according to Stultz, with a bashful bow to Mary, he made a crawfish movement that at last landed him in the street, thence joyfully homeward.

"Well, I can't say as Reuben is a beauty," said John, looking after him with a grin, "but my word for it, Mary, there isn't a better son, nor an honester shopman in this city tonight."

"Don't you think we might go back to tea, father?" asked Mary, for it was just after six o'clock, and this family was not the most fashionable to be found. "The kettle is boiling away finely, and I have set the table all myself."

"Wait a minute, darlin'," he answered, as the doorknob rattled faintly. "There's another little one, you may be sure. Run open the door for the little hands."

Mary quickly obeyed him, and admitted two small ragged specimens of undecided age and sex, the larger of whom marched manfully up to the counter.

"Please, sir, what'll this buy?"

On the very dirty paw extended lay a single worn copper, evidently the large capital of their joint interests. Mr. Pin gazed for a moment at the eager little smutted faces upturned to his, at their garments, then back at his daughter, so neat and fair to see, and suppressing the ready chuckle that ever welled up from his capacious chest, changed it into a peculiar choking sound instead, and then regained speech to ask:

"And what do you want it to buy, my child?"

The two pair of eyes sparkled.

"Kin it buy a cent's worth o' that 'ere thing?"

The bony finger pointed up to a bologna sausage suspended above. The jolly grocer's eyes twinkled at the choice, but muttering a "children will be children," he took it down, cut a long piece off, added to it a handful of crackers, and winding up all with two painted sticks of that candy like a barber's pole which maketh glad the hearts of children, saw the train depart happy as kings, to use a dubious comparison.

Out into the gathering night went, as the door closed again, a gush of light, streaking the pavement and casting still more into obscurity the figure which had never yet stirred from its cramping posture. At this juncture, the eyes set in the wan-like face were glazed with tears as they peered in through the dividing pane. She had wandered far that night from the Asylum that, God help her, the orphan called her home. A shivering dread, like that of a wounded animal, possessed her, of a whipping from the harsh matron upon her return. It had driven her out into the desolate night, but not more lonely than she was in the scene left behind. No voice broke upon her ear—no one came to disturb her. If she were to be found dead that night, they would never ask what caused it. How cold she was!—how bitter, bitter cold! Even that burning pain in the side that had kept her from sleep for so long seemed to grow numb under the paralyzing chill. How nice it must be to be somebody's own little child, and to be kissed sometimes! Nobody had ever kissed her in all her life. Ann did once, when she asked her, but Ann was a big girl and had her work to do. But Ann was kind, for she let her "cuddle up" at night when her side hurt, and her feet got cold.

Christmas bells, holiday bells clanged joyfully out upon the clear, cold air, making the little child start as she drew back her cheek from against the frosty pane. Rockets, with their trail of luminous sparks, darted through the night; crackers and torpedoes sputtered their mimic fires upon the pavement; carriage loads of little children in gala dress, rolled noiselessly over the stones: every house was alight and every heart warmed with the universal holiday.

"Well, I won't shut up just yet," said cheerful Mr. Pin. "Maybe some poor soul'll want to buy a bit of something on their way home. But you and I, Mary, will just go back and sit down to our supper and keep an eye to the shop meanwhile."

Just the cosiest little sitting room in the world that was, with every tin on the dresser (for, with the aid of an adjoining back kitchen, this apartment included parlor and dining room) shining as bright as Mary's willing little hands could help the cook, Cindy, to make them, and reflecting a thousand little leaping flames from the firelight.

"Tomorrow evening, my pet, we'll have the poor neighbors in to drink our healths in good eggnog," said John, when they sat after supper, he in his own armchair, and dear, sober little Mary on his knee, stroking with her velvet hand his silver hair. "Or would you rather have a trip to the theater to celebrate the day?"

Little Mary did not hesitate long. She was one of those natures entirely attuned to the domestic sphere that make the Sabbath of a man's work-day world the perfume of his home, as Mrs. Browning has somewhere given us the idea. And as they drew together pleasant pictures of the morrow's holiday, the bright coal fire sending out its own private jets and rockets all the while, John Pin started up.

"Didn't you hear a child crying, Mary?"

He glanced through the glass door into the shop, and seeing nothing, went to a side window and put his head out. Nothing visible in the alley below under the bank of snow

clouds just beginning to send down their first fluttering tributes, and glancing again through the shop, he saw the knob move weakly. Good John Pin sprang forward fast as his stumpy legs would carry him, and little Mary, looking a perfect Christmas sprite, danced after him. Just there, on the frozen outer step, like a snowflake fallen from the sky, lay the outcast child. Mary suppressed her cry as John Pin, stooping, gathered the tiny burden to his arms and carried it back to the fire. John drew back the hood that had fallen over her face, and saw eyes like faded violets lifted pitifully to his own, and the faint lips part.

"Oh, so cold—so cold!"   .

Tears streamed over Mary's cheeks as she drew forward a lounge and ran for the blankets, while John Pin's rough hands grew tender as a woman's in chafing those small icy fingers, and pouring wine through the thin blue lips. Almost an hour of their loving work had passed before the child spoke again, and then, opening her eyes with a look of quiet intelligence, she said:

"I 'spected you would scold me."

"Scold you, my lamb—not I," answered John Pin cheerfully. "There, now, try and go to sleep, and tomorrow you can tell us all about it."

But the wide open, wondering eyes never closed, and, wandering round the room, rested on the figure of Mary Pin with an air of satisfaction.

"That 'ere looks like the angels," she said, lifting her finger feebly in Mary's direction.

"There's a compliment for you, Mary," said John with a beaming smile.

But Mary did not smile back again. Her young heart was vibrating still with the shock of the hour just past, and a sympathy half divine yet rained its tears upon her face. Gliding up to the child's side, she bent down and kissed the waxen brow, through which the bone showed, oh! so terribly distinct. The child looked up with a smile and nestled to Mary's arm.

"I saw you onst before through the winder. You're prettier than Ann."

John Pin took this occasion to steal off, put up his shutters, close his front door, and go out the back way for a doctor, casting over his shoulder a single look that spoke volumes of love, pity, pride, and heavenly kindness.

"And who is Ann?" asked the older child gently.

"She's the girl that sleeps with me. She's cross sometimes, but onst she kissed me too."

"And how came you away from her to-night?"

" 'Cos I was cold, and the big girls wouldn't let me come to the fire; an' las' night I runned away to look in the shop winders, an' Miss Jane was goin' to whip me tonight when she got time."

"Where do you live, poor child?"

"At the 'Sylum. I was hungry, too, and Sarah Jones stole my bread today, and said she'd call Miss Jane to whip me if I told. Crikey, she's a bad one!"

"Little girl, don't you know you mustn't say such ugly words?"

The child stared. "I hate Sarah, though. She's always skeering me."

"God says we must forgive those who are naughty to us."

The sunken eyes lit up. "Do you know God?" she said eagerly.

"He is my Heavenly Father," answered Mary in her turn, wondering.

"I ain't got no father," the child said, with a look of disappointment. "I thought mebbe you saw him and would ask him to take me up there."

She pointed through the window at the sky. Mary's eyes filled again as she whispered softly:

"He is your Father, too, and will do what you ask him."

"Oh, no, he's not," answered the child decisively. "I never had none. I'm an orphin. Have you got a mother in Heaven too?"

"Yes. My mother went there when I was born."

Mary would have spoken more, but the child's drooping eyelids warned her that she was falling asleep, and presently she slumbered softly upon the other's breast. In this way the Doctor and John Pin found them presently, and after some slight examination and a few whispered words with John, the former went away again. John looked very grave as he came to relieve Mary of her charge, but said nothing.

It was past midnight when the child woke up with a start to meet the gaze of her faithful watchers. For a few minutes she lay quietly, her eyes seemingly attracted by the sprig of holly Mary yet wore.

"May I have that? There's some in the front yard where company walks, but we are whipped if we touches it. Them red things is pretty."

Mary laid the shining leaves and berries beside her, and the child grasped them joyfully.

"Don't let Sarah Jones take 'em," she murmured, falling off to sleep.

All through the night the wind and snow skurried through the streets, making gladsome melody to the safely housed and warmly clad. All through the night, happy children dreamed of the happier morrow; and all through the night that slender thread of life was flowing, flowing.

Day had almost come, when the faint voice again broke the silence of the room.

"My side don't hurt now, and this is warm like Heaven."

"You will be in a much better Heaven soon, little one," said John tenderly.

"Do you want to go to God?" asked Mary's low voice in her deadening ear.

"Will you go too?"

"No, I can't go now, but He will take you if you ask Him. Shall I tell you what to say?"

"Yes, will I go soon?"

"I believe so."

"Then, may I give these to Ann?" lifting the polished leaves.

"Yes; will you ask God now?"

The child lifted herself up in Mary's arms and smiled her faint assent.

"Our Father."

"Our Father."

"Who art in Heaven."

"In—Heaven—"

In Heaven at last!

And the Christmas sunrise broke redly through the panes into the silent room, and the first gleam fell across a tiny waxen form with the holly spray upon its breast.

<hr />

From the *Southern Illustrated News*.

THE SOLDIER COMES HOME

THE SONG OF THE CAMP

BY J. R. M.

FAR away in the piny woods,
　　Where the dews fall heavy and damp,
A soldier sat by the smoldering fire,
　　And sang the song of the camp.

It is not to be weary and worn,
　　It is not to feel hunger and thirst,
It is not the forced march, nor the terrible fight,
　　That seems to the soldier the worst;

But to sit through the comfortless hours,
　　The lonely, dull hours that will come,
With his head in his hands, and his eyes on the
　　　　fire,
　　And his thoughts on visions of home;

To wonder how fares it with those
　　Who mingled so late with his life,
Is it well with my little children three?
　　Is it well with my sickly wife?

This night air is chill, to be sure,
　　But logs lie in plenty around;
How is it with *them* where wood is so dear,
　　And the cash for it hard to be found?

O, that north air cuts bitterly keen,
　　And the ground is hard as a stone;
It would comfort me just to know that they sit
By a fire as warm as my own.

And have they enough to eat?
　　May lads are growing boys,
And my girl is a little tender thing,
　　With her mother's smile and voice.

My wife she should have her tea,
　　Or maybe a sup of beer;
It went to my heart to look on her face,
　　So white, with a smile and a tear.

Her form it is weak and thin,
　　She would gladly work if she could,

But how can a woman have daily strength
　　Who wants for daily food?

My oldest boy *he* can cut wood,
　　And Johnny can carry it in;
But then, how frozen their feet must be
　　If their shoes are worn and thin!

I hope they don't cry with the cold—
　　Are there tears in my little girl's eyes?
O God! say *peace!* to these choking fears,
　　These fears in my heart that rise.

Many rich folks are round them, I know,
　　And their hearts are not hard nor cold,
They would give to my wife if they only know,
　　And my little one three years old.

They would go, like God's angels fair,
　　And enter the lowly door,
And make the sorrowful glad with gifts
　　From their abundant store.

In this blessed Christmastime,
　　When the great gift came to men,
They would show, by their gentle and generous
　　　　deeds,
　　How He cometh in hearts again.

And my sickly, patient wife,
　　And my little children three,
Would be kindly warmed and fed and clothed
　　As part of Christ's family.

Well, I leave it all with God,
　　For my sight is short and dim;
He cares for the falling sparrow;
　　My dear ones are safe with him.

So the soldier watched through the night,
　　Through the dewfall, heavy and damp;
And as he sat by the smoldering fire,
　　He sang the song of the camp.

Holiday Presents.

$7 ARMY WATCH. $10

A BEAUTIFUL ENGRAVED GOLD-PLATED WATCH, Double Case, Lever Cap, Small Size, White Enamelled Dial, Cut Hands, "*English Movements,*" and Correct Timekeeper, with an accurate "*Miniature Calendar,*" indicating the *Day of the Week, Month,* &c., in back case. A single one sent free, by mail, to any address, in neat case, WITH A BEAUTIFUL VEST CHAIN, for only $10.

A neat SILVER WATCH, same as above, with the Miniature Calendar, &c., specially adapted to the ARMY. Sent free by mail, to any address, for only $7.

Address CHAS. P. NORTON & CO., Sole Importers,
o   38 and 40 Ann Street, N. Y.

1863 FIRST PREMIUM AWARDED AT THE STATE FAIRS OF NEW YORK. VERMONT. ILLINOIS. MICHIGAN. IOWA. INDIANA. KENTUCKY. PENNSYLVANIA. OHIO.

GROVER & BAKER'S

HIGHEST PREMIUM ELASTIC STITCH

SEWING MACHINES!

Salesrooms, 495 Broadway, New York.
o

FOR

Holiday Presents,

SEE

J. H. Winslow & Co.'s

The Parlor Ghost.

NOTICE TO THE TRADE.—Now is the time to send in your orders for the greatest sensation of the day.

Every body wants it, and it is just the thing for the Holidays.

THE GREAT NEW HOLIDAY PRIZE PACKET; or,

Santa Claus Christmas Casket.

PRICE ONLY TWENTY-FIVE CENTS.

It contains something for all, both old and young,

And is **Useful, Novel,** and **Amusing.**

In addition to the numerous articles, it contains the receipt for producing, at trifling expense,

THE WONDERFUL PARLOR GHOST.

For sale by all the Wholesale and Retail Stationery and News Dealers throughout the country. Circulars sent free.

THISTLE & CO., 130 Nassau St., N. Y.

The Wonderful Cantering Horses.

Every boy and girl wants one. Prices $14 to $27. Call or send stamp for Circular.
482-3   S. W. SMITH, 498 Broadway.

GOLD $8—SILVER $1.50
1st, 2d, 3d, 4th, 5th, 6th, 9th, 10th, 11th, 12th, 14th, 18th, 20th, 23d

ARMY CORPS,

Showing each Division.

BY THE SINGLE ONE, 100 or 1,000.
Send for Circular.
Address
DROWNE & MOORE,
Manufac'g Jewellers,
208 Broadway, N.Y.

In solid 18 k. gold, $3.50.

Attention, Soldiers!

Every soldier should have a BADGE WITH HIS NAME MARKED DISTINCTLY upon it. The Subscribers will forward to any soldier in the Army a solid Silver Badge, with his Name, Company, and Regiment engraved upon it, on receipt of One Dollar. The above cut represents size and style of Badge furnished. It can be fastened to any garment. Address

DROWNE & MOORE,
Manufacturing Jewelers, 208 Broadway, New York.
N.B.—All kinds of Corps and Co. Pins, Enameled, in Red, White, and Blue, by the one, 100, or 1000.

HOLIDAY GOODS.

Schuyler, Hartley & Graham,

19 Maiden Lane AND 22 John Street,

31 Rue du Chateau d'Eau, Paris, Sands St., Birmingham, England.

French and English Fancy Goods.

PORCELAIN VASES. MANTEL ORNAMENTS. MARBLE CLOCKS. BRONZES. CARD RECEIVERS. PHOTOGRAPH ALBUMS. ODEUR AND DRESSING CASES. CARVED WOOD WORK-BOXES. LIQUER CASES. OPERA GLASSES. FANS. LEATHER BAGS. Also JET AND CORAL JEWELRY, DIAMONDS, WATCHES, &c.

MILITARY GOODS—GUNS—PISTOLS—CUTLERY, &c.
FINE ENGLISH SKATES.

STEEL COLLARS

Enameled White, having all the comforts of linen collars. Washed and dried in a moment. A sample Collar mailed free on receipt of 75 cents. Cuffs $1 00 per pair. Ladies' Collars and Cuffs same price.

WHOLESALE AND RETAIL.

AGENTS WANTED in every Town in the Union.

S. W. H. WARD,

otf   No. 387 Broadway, New York.

American Card Company's New Union Playing Cards.
National Emblems.

Major of Eagles.

The suits are EAGLES, SHIELDS, STARS, and FLAGS. Colonel in place of King; Goddess of Liberty for Queen; Major for Jack.

The Union Playing Cards are the first and only genuine American Cards ever produced, and as they are entered according to Act of Congress, they can be manufactured only by the American Card Company.

The Cards are rapidly taking the place of Cards bearing Foreign emblems. The demand for them is unprecedented in the Card Trade, and they will soon become the Leading Card in the American market.

In playing with these Cards, they are to be called by the names the emblems represent, and as the emblems are as familiar as household words everywhere among the people of the American Republic, they can be used as readily the first occasion as cards bearing Foreign emblems.

The Union Cards are the most pleasing and attractive card ever made. They are produced in the highest style of the art, and each pack is put up in an elegant Card Case, suitable to keep them in when not in use, and then in handsome dozen boxes for the trade.

Two Sample Packs in Card Cases sent, post-paid, on receipt of $1.

Address AMERICAN CARD COMPANY,
455 Broadway, or 165 William St., N. Y.

Cavalry Badges

Constantly on hand and Engraved to Order, and sent free on receipt of Price.

Terms Cash in advance. Send for a Catalogue. Address C. L. BALCH & CO., 208 Broadway, New York.

SERPENTS DE PHARAON;
OR,
SERPENT'S EGGS.

The latest scientific miracle.
"Truly marvelous and apparently inexhaustible"—London Times.

Wholesale and retail by
OLDEN & SAWYER, 246 Canal St., New York.
Fifty cents a box, free by mail. Liberal Discount to the Trade. AGENTS WANTED.

Parr's Tool Chests, fitted with complete sets of Tools, sharpened and set ready for use, and packed in cases for shipping.

Prices from $2 to $35 each, and containing from 8 to 92 Tools, according to size.

Shipped on receipt of price. Send for descriptive circular to the manufacturer.

GEO. PARR, Buffalo, N. Y.

Musical Boxes,

Playing 1, 2, 3, 4, 6, 8, 10, 12, 16, 24, and 36 tunes, and costing from $2 75 to $450 00. A beautiful article for HOLIDAY PRESENTS. My stock of Musical Boxes is the ONLY complete one to be found in this country M. J. PAILLARD, Importer, No. 21 Maiden Lane (up stairs), New York.

LINCOLN AND TAD

CHRISTMAS IN THE WHITE HOUSE

BY JULIA TAFT BAYNE

SATURDAY MORNING, at our house, was devoted to a study of the Sunday school lesson. Willie and Tad appeared early, as they always did. The Lincoln boys had enrolled themselves with my brothers in the Sunday school of our church, the Fourth Presbyterian.

It was December and cold. Willie and Tad had been talking of winters in Illinois, of skating and sledding and snowballing. My Washington-bred brothers listened with round eyes. They possessed no mittens, no sled, no skates. They had never known the delights of a real snowstorm.

Tad dashed at the Sabbath questions with the cheerful audacity characteristic of him. Willie sighed as he said that there were more hard words than ever in it.

The very youngest son of the family, Willie Taft, being what Tad called a "Sunday-school infant" and not required to study any lesson, sat curled up on the window seat.

The older boys studied with set, determined looks. There were several bits of catechism deftly interpolated; and in our Sunday school these must be recited verbatim. Tad and Holly wriggled and fidgeted, repeating the lines in a loud whisper, each gradually departing from the text and copying the other's mistakes until they had to begin all over again.

The infant scholar in the window also diverted attention by proclaiming at intervals. "There's a dwunk man walking the beat with a log," or "Here comes the officer of the day; they're turning out the guard." Again it would be, "I fink there's a hundred Army mules up the street fighting right smart."

Tad paused in the murmur of "the moral law—the moral law—" to ask, "Julie, what is a mud sill?"

"Never mind, Tad, go on. 'The moral law is summarily comprehended—' "

"But, what is it?"

"Why, a Yankee, Tad."

"Well, a boy in Lafayette Square said we were 'em, and we am not."

"Of course not," said Willie Lincoln. "Every-body knows they come from Connecticut."

"Bud and Willie wouldn't let me punch him 'cause they said it would be put in the papers, but I will if he says it again."

It was still cold and wet and blustering. Only an occasional officer rode past, his great cape over his head. The boys watched the gusts of rain anxiously. They had been promised a ride with the staff if it was not too stormy.

My cousin, a tall young captain . . . came and leaned against the doorway and sympathetically confessed that he himself had to learn the Commandments and Creed before the morrow's morn.

"What for?" demanded the boys, astonished that the shoulder-strapped six-footer should still be in thralldom to the blue question book.

"Because we have a Sunday school in the defenses, and the colonel is superintendent."

"Snow! snow!" shouted Tad, as some light flakes flew by the window. "That's what I like better'n anything. I hope it'll be over the fences."

Tad's wish was futile. To his great disappointment the snowflakes grew more and more infrequent, and at last the sun shone out. The boys went off, hopeful of a ride at least.

About noon a relative arrived unexpectedly. As he had to go to his command that evening and wished to see the children, I was sent to find the boys and bring them home. I went at once to the White House and looked outside first; the grounds, the stable, the conservatory; then the kitchen, where I learned that the boys had an early lunch and had not been seen since. The ride with the staff had not materialized, and the Madam had gone for a drive but had not taken the boys.

I ran up into the sitting room and almost collided with the tall form of the President, who was crossing the room on the way to his office. He had some papers in one hand and with the other he stopped my flight, saying, "Here, here, flibbertigibbet, where are you going in such a hurry?"

"I am looking for the boys and I cannot find them anywhere. Cousin Sam Andrus is at our house with a colonel. I forget his name but he is awfully nice."

"Awfully nice, is he?" said Mr. Lincoln, with the quizzical smile I remember so well.

"Yes, sir, and they want to see the boys, ours and yours, Willie and Tad, you know."

"Yes, I know. Have you looked in the attic, Julie?"

"I'm going there now," I said, and left him watching my headlong progress toward the attic, with that same smile on his face.

In the attic was a large bin of visiting cards, which apparently had been lately disturbed, as there was a nest hollowed out in the center, and the cards were scattered all around the floor. But the boys were not there; so I went home and reported.

After dinner, as the men were enjoying their cigars . . . the four boys appeared, dragging a remarkable object which consisted mainly of an old chair on barrel staves and the cover of a Congressional Record nailed to the broken seat. This, they proudly informed us, was a snow sled.

Holly hung back as they were severally presented to the colonel, and Tad triumphantly explained that "Holly burned an awful hole in his pants with powder out of a cartridge given him by a soldier who said it wouldn't go off."

Both Tad and Holly were very uneasy and continually rubbed against the veranda railing. When questioned by mother, Tad said, "I s'pose it's the snowballs we've got down our backs."

"Snowballs," said mother, surprised. "Where did you find any snow?"

"Up in our attic," said Tad. "Handfuls and handfuls and bushels and bushels."

Naturally we all looked amazed at this statement until Willie explained. "Why, Mama Taft, Tad's snow is cards. There are bushels in our attic in a big bin and we throw them up and play it's snowing. There are all the cards all the people have left on the Presidents since General Washington."

"General Washington never lived in your house," said Bud. "The tutor said he didn't."

"Well, there's enough to make a snowstorm without his," said Willie.

"And Tad and Holly stuffed them down each other's backs like real snow, but I guess they're sharp cornered and sticky."

"Yes," said Tad; "they stick to you, and they stick into you."

Declaring they couldn't stand it another minute, Holly and Tad went upstairs, Tad calling back, "Next time we'll pour the snow on the attic stairs and slide down on our snow sled."

The next morning, going into the boys' room, I saw in the middle of the card-strewn floor the name of Jenny Lind, the great singer. So I picked up this card, and then another and another, as they interested me, leaving many to be swept up by the maid.

And here are some snowflakes from Tad Lincoln's snowstorm:

From *Tad Lincoln's Father* by Julia Taft Bayne. Boston, 1931.

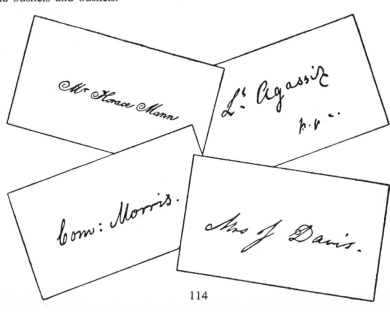

Frederick Hill Meserve Collection

ABRAHAM LINCOLN

ABRAHAM LINCOLN'S
LAST CHRISTMAS

BY PHILIP VAN DOREN STERN

FROST laced the edges of the windowpanes, vignetting the bleak winter landscape. Snow does queer things to places, he thought. In the twilight, the wide mud flats near the ice-covered Potomac looked like the Illinois prairies, and the Virginia hills on the other side of the river might be the Kentucky mountains he had known as a boy. Winter sounds were the same everywhere. A guard marching up and down under the White House windows crunched the hard, frozen snow crystals under his boot; some boys playing in the meadows near the river were shouting—their voices were brittle in the cold air. They were familiar sounds that brought back many memories.

A man in his fifties remembers many Christmases. Worst of all had been the one during that first terrible winter in Illinois when his family had been snowed in for weeks in the hastily built cabin on a bluff above the Sangamon. They had stayed in bed eighteen hours a day to keep warm and to forget their hunger by sleeping as much as they could. He shivered when he thought of that desolate cabin where even the firewood had to be used sparingly because it was almost impossible to go out in the shoulder-deep snow to get more. But he smiled wistfully when he recalled the gingerbread man his stepmother made for him every Christmas during the hard years in Indiana.

Yes, a man in his fifties remembers many Christmases. There was that awful day in New Salem when he had walked for miles to a lonely country cemetery to brush the snow away from Ann's grave. He could never bear the thought of the rain falling on her, and the snow was even worse. Yet it must be lying deep there now on that deserted hill, and there was no one to brush it away. It was lying on so many graves—thousands and tens of thousands of them made during the last four years.

But all his Christmases had not been so bad. He remembered the first one after Robert had been born. Mary had lighted a candle at the foot of the cradle before there was any sign of dawn in the sky, and the waking child had crowed with delight when he saw the yellow flame. They had stood beside the cradle while the shabby room that was their temporary home lightened with the coming of day.

And then, during the later years, after the other three children had come, the big house in Springfield had resounded with their shouts and laughter each Christmas morning. Some day they would return there, after all this was over. But only two of the children would be with them. He forced his mind away from those unhappiest of all times. Bob would be home from Harvard for Christmas, and Tad would soon be coming in to say good night in his odd childish lisp.

He left the window and walked slowly toward the long table piled with papers and reports, knowing that he had to take up the business of the day. Word should be arriving soon from Sherman, whose ever-advancing army had reached Savannah and the sea. The war could not last much longer now. The coming year might see it over, and then there would be the complicated problems of peace to face. Sometimes he thought he dreaded them more than he did the war. He sat down wearily in his big chair at the head of the cabinet table and called out to Billy Slade.

The old colored manservant opened the door noiselessly and came in to light the gas. In the growing light, the long white room took on shape and became more cheerful. Billy told him that Gideon Welles, his Secretary of the Navy, was waiting to see him.

"Send him in," he said gladly. He knew why Welles had come. There would be Christmas pardons to sign, and his face brightened.

Secretary of the Navy Welles entered, his long white beard making him look oddly like Santa Claus. He seemed quite embarrassed, as he always did under such circumstances. He thought it a weakness on the part of the President to grant pardons so easily, yet he aided and abetted him, even going over Stanton's head to see that they reached his attention.

"I have some papers for you to sign," he began in a brisk voice. "Christmas pardons. We've discussed most of them already. You'll remember this case, I'm sure." He deftly slipped a sheet of paper covered with writing in front of the man at the table. The President put on his glasses and nodded when he recognized the case. "You agreed to commute the sentence," Welles said, speaking rapidly as if to ward off argument. "It's a routine matter now, needing only your signature to make it official."

The President reached for his pen, wondering whether the commutation of a death sentence could ever be a routine matter. He marveled, as always, at the power that flowed from the fine steel point. The words "A. Lincoln" would set unseen wheels in motion; telegraph wires would carry the good news to a distant family; and somewhere a boy in a prison cell would be told that he did not have to die. He glanced at his signature with pleasure. There were some advantages in being President—especially on Christmas Eve.

Then Welles gave him other pardons to sign. When they were duly inscribed and dated, the august-looking Secretary of the Navy stood anxiously folding and refolding a small sheet of letter paper that was obviously not an official document.

"I have a favor to ask, sir," he said hesitatingly. "Or rather Mrs. Welles has. It's a bit difficult to explain." His eyes wandered to the burning gas jets, and his voice died away. The President waited patiently.

"It has to do with a Rebel female," Welles blurted out at last.

"A Rebel female?"

"Yes, sir. A friend of my wife."

Welles stood shifting about unhappily under the President's gaze. "I know what you're thinking, sir. That the family of a Cabinet officer shouldn't have such friends. We don't make a practice of it, but this case is different."

Lincoln's expression was quizzical. He leaned back in his chair and put his finger tips together. "And what does this Rebel female want?" he asked in an amused voice.

"Well, to put it bluntly, sir—she wants to get married."

Lincoln grinned. "She doesn't need my help for that. There's no law forbidding marriage —even for Rebel females. Whom does she want to marry?"

"That's just the trouble, sir. Some Rebel whelp in Richmond. She can't get through the lines."

"So you want me to give her a pass?"

Welles nodded vigorously.

"Has she taken the oath of allegiance?"

Welles frowned. "I've talked to her—and so has my wife. But she's stubborn. I regret to say that she refuses to take the oath. Says she owes her allegiance to Virginia, and not to the United States."

"Yet you want me to grant her a pass. That might be interpreted by some as giving aid and comfort to the enemy."

"Yes, sir, it might," Welles said grimly.

"But you still want me to do it?"

"I don't think it would do any great harm, sir. We have never recognized the Confederacy, so Virginia is still part of this country. There

still have to be marriages—and children. We have to think of the future. The nation has been seriously depopulated by this war."

"Perhaps you'd better tell me more about this Rebel female," the President said quietly. He motioned toward a chair. Welles sat down uneasily, spreading out the letter which he had folded so often that it looked like an accordion pleat. He glanced at it with surprise as if he had never seen it before.

"She came here at the beginning of the war," Welles began. "Her mother was sick, and she had to take care of her. The mother died, so she's been stranded here ever since. As she says herself, the years of her youth are passing away. She's nearly four years older now, and—"

"Just how old is she?"

"I don't know for certain, sir. About twenty-three, I'd say."

"H-m. Twenty-three. Practically superannuated for a Southern girl. We'll have to do something about it, Mr. Welles."

"I suggest you read her own statement first. It's rather intemperate, I'm sorry to say." He handed the letter to the President, who laid it face down on the table and shook his head.

"I'd rather not read it," he said, smiling. "It might prejudice my decision. Tell me more about her. Who is she, and where is she now?"

"Her name is Laura Jones—and she's sitting right outside the door this minute."

The President looked startled. "Does she want to talk to me?"

"She said she ought to be here in case you wanted to talk to her." He studied the President's face. "Do you?"

"I don't think it will be necessary. But I would like to see what she looks like. You can tell a great deal from a person's face."

Welles stood up and asked rather doubtfully, "How do you want to arrange it?"

"You might go out to ask her some question," the President suggested. "You could leave the door open accidentally."

Welles' face was properly sober as he went to the door. Before he reached it, the President spoke again. "And then you might find some errand down the hall to keep you busy for a minute. I want to get a good look at her."

The girl in the visitor's chair half arose when

she saw the impressive-looking figure of the Secretary of the Navy advancing toward her. He motioned to her to remain seated and spoke to her in a whisper. Then he was gone, padding softly down the hallway.

They sat looking at each other through the doorway for a long moment, the aging man at the Cabinet table and the young Confederate girl who had refused to take an oath of allegiance to his government. They were supposed to be enemies, he thought sadly. Her people and his were engaged in a death struggle on battlefields that covered half the nation. Yet she was as American as he was, both citizens of a republic that had been born in war and revolution. The state of Virginia to which she gave fierce allegiance had provided Washington and Jefferson as his predecessors in office. They had many things in common, she and he, and not the least of them was the heritage Virginia had given the nation.

Hostility between them was unthinkable, he decided. His eyes sought her written statement, but he pushed it resolutely away. When he glanced up at her again, he saw that she was smiling at him.

Her thin, forlorn face was transformed. He was tempted to get up and speak to her, but he heard Welles' footsteps coming down the hallway. He sank back in his chair and assumed a stern, Presidential look. The girl was murmuring something to Welles. A moment later the secretary entered the room and closed the door behind him.

"What do you think, sir!" Welles asked.

"I think she should be allowed to return to Richmond."

Welles smiled. "I thought you would. But don't you want to read her statement first? She makes no bones about her Rebel sentiments."

The President picked up the sheet of paper lying before him on the table and deliberately tore it into pieces. Then he took his pen and wrote out a pass. "I don't suppose it matters if I date this tomorrow?" Without waiting for a reply, he wrote the words, "Christmas Day, December 25, 1864," and appended his signature to the document.

"That makes it a Christmas present," he said, handing it to Welles.

His Secretary of the Navy bowed and put the paper carefully in his pocket. "I thank you, sir," he said gravely. "The young lady just whispered something to me which I think I may repeat." He cleared his throat. "She said you weren't at all like the monster you had been pictured. She said you reminded her of her father. And she wished you a very merry Christmas."

"You told her I was going to sign the pass?"

"Yes, sir." Welles' face was expressionless. "I didn't have any doubt of it—even from the beginning." He bowed again and went to the door. "Mrs. Welles and I wish you a very merry Christmas, sir. A very merry Christmas and many of them."

He shut the door silently and was gone. The President got up from the table and went to the window. It was dark outside now, and there was a faint glow of light on the snow from the gas lamps on the lower floor. He could hear the steady crunching of the guard's boots. Somewhere a church bell was ringing, calling worshipers to vespers on Christmas Eve.

Yes, a man in his fifties remembers many Christmases. What was it the girl had said? "The years of my youth are passing away." They had already passed for him, he knew. Suddenly he felt very old, as though he had lived out all his life and there was nothing left. In a few weeks he would be fifty-six. He had seen many Christmases come and go, three of them in the White House—and tomorrow would be the fourth. But by this time next year, the war should be over. In another four years, he and Mary could return to Springfield to stay there in peace.

As he stood looking out at the darkness, the melancholy that had haunted him all his life returned. The brief glow of happiness the Christmas pardons had given him was gone.

The frost was riming the windowpanes again, reaching out with icy fingers to shut the world away. His hands and legs felt cold, as they so often did these days. He shivered. Tomorrow would be his fifty-sixth Christmas. How many Christmases could a man in his fifties expect to see?

From *Collier's*, December 26, 1942.

CHRISTMAS·DINNER

MENUS FOR CHRISTMAS AND
NEW YEAR'S DINNERS

Boiled turkey with oyster sauce, roast goose with apple sauce, roasted ham, chicken pie, stewed beets, coleslaw, turnips, salsify, winter squash; mince pie, plum pudding, lemon custards, cranberry pie.

Roast turkey with cranberry sauce, boiled fowls with celery sauce, boiled ham, goose pie, turnips, salsify, coleslaw, winter squash,

beets; mince pudding boiled, lemon pudding baked, pumpkin pudding.

Mock turtle soup, roast turkey with cranberry sauce, boiled turkey with celery sauce, roasted ham, smoked tongue, chicken curry, oyster pie, beets, coleslaw, winter squash, salsify, fried·celery; plum pudding, mince pie, calf's-foot jelly, blanc mange.

RECEIPTS FOR CHRISTMAS

THE PHILOSOPHY OF PLUM PUDDINGS. In the making of plum puddings, the following results of the examination and comparison of eighteen receipts may be usefully studied and applied:

Average of Eighteen Receipts for Plum Pudding. Fine flour, half a pound; bread crumbs, quarter of a pound; suet, three-quarters of a pound; eggs (yolk and white), four; mixed dried fruit, one pound and a half; mixed liquid, a third of a pint.

Average Deductions Respecting the Composition. A classification of the receipts gives the following independent dogmas, namely, that when a plum pudding contains

Less flour, it must have more egg, bread crumb, and fruit.

Less egg, it must have more flour and less liquid.

Less bread crumb, it must have more flour and liquid and less suet.

Less suet, it must have less bread crumb and fruit.

Less fruit, it must have less egg and suet, with more flour.

Less liquid, it must have less egg and more bread crumb.

With respect to the mixing of the ingredients, different modes are employed. The eggs are always beat up previously in a separate state; and the milk, spice, flour, and crumbs are generally added by degrees, and beat up successively, adding the suet and fruit next, and the brandy last. In some cases, however, this process is reversed, and the eggs are added last; but, in general, the eggs and milk, the flour, suet and fruit, and the spices, go together. The pudding bag is always well dredged with flour, and often tied rather loosely that the pudding may swell; and, after boiling it, about five minutes are suffered to elapse in order that the moisture may evaporate from the outside of the cloth and allow it to leave the pudding in a perfect state. Some are boiled in a cloth only, some in a mould only, with a cloth over the mouth, and others in both a cloth and basin. They all should have pounded white sugar sprinkled freely over them on being served on the dish for table.

Much puzzling difference is apparent in the time directed for the boiling of the puddings of each receipt. This appears to depend on the nature of the composition and the proportion of binding material. We have instituted a comparison of all the receipts by reducing the weight of ingredients to the average standard, and have obtained the following independent deductions:

1. Plum puddings require the *same* boiling if the crumb be left out and more flour, egg, and fruit supply its place.

2. They require *more* boiling when containing a greater proportion of flour and egg, but less crumb and suet, or when boiled in a mould.

3. They require *less* boiling when having less flour but more crumb and fruit.

4. The average time of boiling for ingredients weighing four pounds is about four hours.

CHRISTMAS PLUM PUDDING. A pound of suet, cut in pieces not too fine, a pound of currants, and a pound of raisins stoned, four eggs, half a grated nutmeg, an ounce of citron and lemon peel, shred fine, a teaspoonful of beaten ginger, half a pound of bread crumbs, half a pound of flour, and a pint of milk. Beat the eggs first, add half the milk, beat them together, and by degrees stir in the flour, then the suet, spice and fruit, and as much milk as will mix it together very thick. Then take a clean cloth, dip in boiling water, and squeeze dry. While the water is boiling fast, put in your pudding, which should boil at least five hours.

Another way. Seven ounces raisins, seeded and a little chopped; seven ounces currants, well washed and picked; one and a half ounce citron; three ounces beef suet chopped very fine; three-quarters of a nutmeg grated; one-quarter of a teaspoonful of cinnamon; five eggs well beaten up; four tablespoonfuls of sugar; five tablespoonfuls of wheat flour; half a lemon peel grated; one glass of brandy and one glass of Madeira; a little milk to mix, sufficient to make rather a thick batter. The whole must be well mixed. The above mixture to be put into a well-buttered basin. Tie a pudding cloth over, and pin the four corners over the top. Put into boiling water, and to be kept boiling without ceasing for five hours. We have tried this receipt, and know it to be excellent.

RICH PLUM PUDDING. Stone carefully one pound of the best raisins, wash and pick one pound of currants, chop very small one pound of fresh beef suet, blanch and chop small or pound two ounces of sweet almonds and one ounce of bitter ones; mix the whole well together, with one pound of sifted flour, and the same weight of crumb of bread soaked in milk, then squeezed dry and stirred with a spoon until reduced to a mash, before it is mixed with the flour. Cut in small pieces two ounces each of preserved citron, orange, and lemon peel, and add a quarter of an ounce of mixed spice; quarter of a pound of moist sugar should be put into a basin with eight eggs, and well beaten together with a three-pronged fork. Stir this with the pudding, and make it of a proper consistence with milk. Remember that it must not be made too thin, or the fruit will sink to the bottom, but be made to the consistence of good thick batter. Two wineglassfuls of brandy should be poured over the fruit and spice, mixed together in a basin, and allowed to stand three or four hours before the pudding is made, stirring occasionally. It must be tied in a cloth, and will take five hours of constant boiling. When done, turn it out on a dish, sift loaf sugar over the top, and serve it with wine sauce in a boat, and some poured round the pudding. The pudding will be of considerable size, but half the quantity of materials, used in the same proportion, will be equally good.

A GOOD CHRISTMAS PUDDING. One pound of flour, two pounds of suet, one pound of currants, one pound of plums, eight eggs, two ounces of candied peel, almonds and mixed spice according to taste. Boil gently for seven hours.

MINCEMEAT. Six pounds of currants, three pounds of raisins stoned, three pounds of apples chopped fine, four pounds of suet, two pounds of sugar, two pounds of beef, the peel and juice of two lemons, a pint of sweet wine, a quarter of a pint of brandy, half an ounce of mixed spice. Press the whole into a deep pan when well mixed.

Another way. Two pounds of raisins, three pounds of currants, three pounds of beef suet, two pounds of moist sugar, two ounces of citron, one ounce of orange peel, one small nutmeg, one pottle of apples chopped fine, the rind of two lemons and juice of one, half a pint of brandy. Mix well together. This should be made a little time before wanted for use.

MINCE PIES. Take a pound of beef, free from skin and strings, and chop it very fine. Then two pounds of suet, which likewise pick and chop. Then add three pounds of currants nicely cleaned and perfectly dry, one pound and a half of apples, the peel and juice of a lemon, half a pint of sweet wine, half a nutmeg, and a few cloves and mace, with pimento in fine powder. Have citron, orange and lemon peel ready, and put some in each of the pies when made.

TURKEY

TO ROAST A TURKEY: Prepare a stuffing of pork sausage-meat, one beaten egg, and a few crumbs of bread; or if sausages are to be served with the turkey, stuffing as for fillet of veal; in either, a little shred shallot is an improvement. Stuff the bird under the breast; dredge it with flour, and put it down to a clear, brisk fire; at a moderate distance the first half hour, but afterwards nearer. Baste with butter; and when the turkey is plumped up, and the steam draws towards the fire, it will be nearly done; then dredge it lightly with flour, and baste it with a little more butter, first melted in the basting ladle. Serve with gravy in the dish and bread sauce in a tureen. It may be garnished with sausages, or with fried force-meat, if veal stuffing be used. Sometimes the gizzard and liver are dipped into the yolk of an egg, sprinkled with salt and Cayenne, and then put under the pinions before the bird is put to the fire. A very large turkey will require three hour's roasting; one of eight or ten pounds, two hours; and a small one, an hour and a half. Roasted chestnuts, grated or sliced, and green truffles, sliced, are excellent additions to the stuffing for turkeys.

121

To Boil a Turkey: Make a stuffing as for veal; or if you wish a plain stuffing, pound crackers or breadcrumbs very fine, chop raw salt pork very fine, sift some sage and any other sweet herbs that are liked, season with pepper, and mold them together with the yolk of an egg; put this under the breast, and tie it closely. Set the turkey in boiling water enough to cover it; boil very slowly, and take off the scum as it rises. A large turkey will require more than two hours' boiling; a small one an hour and a half. Garnish with fried forcemeat, and serve with oyster or celery sauce.

OR: Fill the body with oysters, and let it boil by steam without any water. When sufficiently done, take it up, strain the gravy that will be found in the pan, and which, when cold, will be a fine jelly; thicken it with a little flour and butter, add the liquor of the oysters intended for sauce, also stewed, and warm the oysters up in it; whiten it with a little boiled cream, and pour it over the turkey.

From *Godey's Lady's Book* for December, 1862.

A LEAN BILL OF FARE OF SUBSTITUTE FOODS FOR A CONFEDERATE CHRISTMAS

The matrons had a . . . difficult problem to solve in answering the question: "What shall we eat and drink?" The economy they practiced, the devices they resorted to to swell their menu would fill volumes.

Wheat, rye, corn, and chestnuts were used as substitutes for Java and Mocha. Sassafras and other herbs were infused as teas. These were sweetened with brown or maple sugar. Molasses and strained honey were in demand for putting up fruit and manufacturing conserves. Sorghum, made from the Chinese sugarcane, was an acrid syrup in high favor at the table, and for making black and ginger cakes. Very frequently these cookies were called ginger merely in compliment. Spices were hard to obtain and often of most in-

different quality. Dried fruits were our great standby, as these could be preserved without sugar. Molasses and apple pies formed our great rallying point wherever the question of dessert presented itself to our vexed minds. Doughnuts were great favorites with the soldiers, and the best our boards afforded were always set before them. Buttermilk was a favorite draught; cornbread pones baked in a Dutch oven took the place of sweetened puddings. Eggs and butter were often scarce and impossible to buy in the winter season.

At Christmas our skill was taxed to the utmost to spread the festal board as in days before the war. The smoking turkey was there, but where were the generous dishes that flanked it in days of yore! The flaming plum pudding, the rich fruit cake, the spicy mince pie. We substituted black cake and molasses, or suet pudding with sauce. Dried currants took the place of raisins, and home-made wines of claret and Madeira. . . .

Confederate receipt books aided us in the simplification of household economy. They were small pamphlets bound in coarse brown paper, and containing not a few useful hints for the distressed housekeeper, such as a receipt for making apple pie without apples by substituting crackers soaked in water and flavored with citric acid.

Lemons and oranges came to us from Florida, and goobers and pecans from the Carolinas and Georgia. In summer we lived upon a vegetable and fruit diet, but in winter, corn bread and pork formed the bulk of our living. The country people fared better than those living in the cities, who were dependent upon the market. A roast potato or bowl of mush and milk often formed our bill of fare for supper in the hard season.

THE FIRST PEACETIME CHRISTMAS

December 25, 1865

THE WAR WAS OVER, and peace had come at last. But Christmas that year was marred by a tremendous gale which swept along the Atlantic coast on December 20, wrecking many ships and drowning some of the people who had ventured to sea on them.

In New York, the weather was still bad on Christmas Eve. Rain, slush, and snow kept many at home who otherwise would have gone to church or visited friends and relatives. The weather spoiled the skating too, which had been good early in the month. Fortunately, the weather cleared on Christmas Day, although the rain had melted all the snow.

Turkeys sold at $.28 a pound; prime beef brought $.35. These were high prices for the time, inflated as a result of the war. But there was plenty of food. The markets were filled with heaps of venison, suckling pigs, canvasback ducks, geese, chickens, quail, prairie hens, partridges, and the now-extinct wild pigeons. The demand was good—much better than it had been the year before.

Because Christmas Eve occurred on Sunday, the customary public celebrations were postponed to Monday night. In New York, the Santa Claus Association opened its Christmas Ball with a quadrille followed by waltzes, polkas, galops, lancers, and schottisches.

Everyone was very much aware of the difference between this Christmas and the one the year before; even the newspapers commented editorially on it. But the nation was not only at peace; it had also gone through a social upheaval which was to change its structure forever.

Just a week before Christmas, on Monday, December 18, Secretary of State Seward had made an official announcement of major importance. Lincoln's Emancipation Proclamation was a war measure that declared the slaves to be free only in the seceded states. There was some doubt of the legal validity of this in peacetime, and to settle such doubt Congress had passed the Thirteenth Amendment to the Constitution on February 1, 1865. Illinois, Lincoln's own state, was the first to ratify it. Then other states followed, one by one, until the necessary three-fourths (27 out of 36) of all the states had ratified the proposed Amendment. The wording of the Thirteenth Amendment was couched in language that was older than the Constitution itself, for it was based on phrases used in the ordinance of July 13, 1787, which had created the Northwest Territory where slavery was specifically forbidden. The new Amendment (the first to be passed since 1804) stated that: "Neither slavery nor involuntary servitude, except as a punishment for crime whereof the party shall have been duly convicted, shall exist within the United States, or any place subject to their jurisdiction.

With the ratification of the Thirteenth Amendment, the war that had just been fought took on new meaning. It had not only preserved the Union but had abolished slavery as well. The promises made in the Declaration of Independence on July 4, 1776, had at last been made good. "We hold these truths to be self-evident, that all men are created equal, that they are endowed by their Creator with certain unalienable Rights, that among these are Life, Liberty, and the pursuit of Happiness."

On Christmas 1865, the nation, no longer divided, celebrated for the first time a new birth of freedom in the land.

CHRISTMAS SHOPPERS AT NEW YORK'S WASHINGTON MARKET

BUYING THE CHRISTMAS TURKEY

LET us talk of buying the Christmas turkey. Pockets are prepared for it, brains are dwelling upon it, and mouths are watering for it. Country people are counting upon it, and viewing with calm complacency their flocks of gobblers, and calculating keenly upon the probable price of turkey flesh upon the Christmas Eve. The hucksters are sweeping up their stalls and making ready every available inch of room to store the stock they expect to have on hand. Railroads are getting ready extra trains to bring in the loads and tons of turkey that will be required by this insatiable metropolitan maw, and housewives are looking up the thyme and summer savory they put by to dry last fall, to make up the stuffing.

And then all through the day and the night of Christmas Eve, how every market and every store where the delicious bird is sold will be filled. How they will be viewed with critical eyes, and felt with suspicious fingers, for what heavier misfortune could fall upon a housekeeper than to present a tough turkey on the home table on Christmas Day? Preserve all our friends from that terrible trouble! How the market man will expatiate on their excellencies. How he will point out their plump points, and show off the tenderness of the breast bone, and the easy crack of the wings. How he will, unsuccessfully, endeavor to convince the buyer that twenty-five cents per pound for turkey is dirt cheap, and that by fair rights, seeing that there is only twice as much in the city as is really wanted, turkey ought to be fifty cents a pound. Ah! the wonderful eloquence of these market men, who can make black white, and send off a guileless customer with exactly what he don't want at exactly thirty-three per cent more than it is worth. It is wonderful.

And now the turkey is bought, a sound fourteen-pounder, perhaps, for there may be a family of as many to feed, including poor relations, for it will not do to run short, and a pound apiece is tolerable rations, providing the accompaniments, such as vegetables, a few oysters, cranberry sauce, and mince pies or pudding, are plentiful. The turkey is bought, stuffed, roasted and on table; the company is gathered, and paterfamilias takes his stand at the head of the table, the knife is flourished,

PEACE AT LAST, CHRISTMAS, 1865

The markets are filled with fine foods and delicacies for eager shoppers.

the fork is plunged, the rich gravy flows, the joints fall, slices of white breast are watched greedily by the hungry party, plate after plate goes away from the table head, there is stillness only broken by the clatter of a dozen knives and forks, or the almost audible gnashing of teeth, and—oh! but our pen fails us here, and we *must* close.

From *Leslie's Weekly*, December 30, 1865.

125

AFTER THE WAR WAS OVER—

CHRISTMAS MORNING, 1865

THE EDITOR AND HIS BOOK

Philip Van Doren Stern has been a frequent contributor to magazines and journals and a prolific book author and editor since 1932. He is also a well-known and widely-respected authority on the American Civil War. Born September 10, 1900, in Wyalusing, Pennsylvania, he graduated from Rutgers University in 1924 (Litt. B.) and received an honorary degree (Litt. D.) from that institution in 1940. From 1924 to 1933 he worked in the advertising field. Since 1933, he has been connected with publishing, including serving as General Manager for Editions for the Armed Services from 1943 to 1945. In 1928, he married the former Lillian Diamond. They live in Brooklyn, New York, and have one daughter, Marguerite Louise. Mr. Stern is an excellent photographer, a Hi-Fi enthusiast, and an avid collector of Civil War books.

Among the many books which Mr. Stern has written, the following are the most outstanding: *An Introduction to Typography* (Harper, 1932); *Love Is The One With Wings* (Farrar, Straus, 1951); *A Pictorial History of the Automobile* (Viking, 1953); *Tin Lizzie* (Simon and Schuster, 1955); *The Greatest Gift* (McKay, 1944); *The Man Who Killed Lincoln* (Random House, 1939); *The Drums of Morning* (Doubleday, 1942); *An End to Valor* (Houghton Mifflin, 1958); *They Were There* (Crown, 1959); *Lola* (Rinehart, 1949); and *Our Constitution* (Birk and Company, 1953). Among the many books which Mr. Stern has edited, the following are the best known: *Pocket Book of Modern American Short Stories* (Pocket Books); *The Portable Library Poe* (Viking, 1945); *The Breathless Moment* (with Herbert Asbury, Knopf, 1935); *The Selected Works of De Quincey* (Random House, 1937); *The Midnight Reader* (Holt, 1942); *The Moonlight Traveler* (Doubleday, 1943); *The Holiday Reader* (with Bernard Smith, Simon and Schuster, 1947); *Travelers in Time* (Doubleday, 1947); *The Life and Writings of Abraham Lincoln* (Random House, 1940); *The Assassination of President Lincoln and the Trial of the Conspirators* (Funk, 1954); *Secret Missions of the Civil War* (Rand McNally, 1959); *The Secret Service of the Confederate States in Europe* (by James D. Bulloch, Yoseloff, 1959); *Wearing of the Gray* (by John Esten Cooke, Indiana, 1959); *My Father, General Lee* (by Robert E. Lee, Jr., Doubleday, 1960); *General Lee* (by Fitzhugh Lee, Fawcett, 1961); *Soldier Life in the Union and Confederate Armies* (Indiana University Press, 1961); and *Prologue to Sumter* (Indiana University Press, 1961).

THE CIVIL WAR CHRISTMAS ALBUM (Hawthorn, 1961) was designed by Sidney Feinberg. The body type is Times Roman, originally designed for use by *The Times* of London. Type was set by Pyramid Composition Company, Inc., New York City. The book was printed by lithography by Halliday Lithograph Corporation, West Hanover, Massachusetts. It was bound by the Montauk Book Manufacturing Co., Inc., New York City.

A HAWTHORN BOOK

DATE DUE

GAYLORD

PRINTED IN U.S.A.